Stephen Crane

Also by Mark Sufrin
George Catlin: Painter of the Indian West

94-265

Stephen Crane

by Mark Sufrin

ATHENEUM   1992   New York

Maxwell Macmillan Canada
Toronto

Maxwell Macmillan International
New York   Oxford   Singapore   Sydney

Atheneum
Macmillan Publishing Company
866 Third Avenue
New York, NY 10022

Maxwell Macmillan Canada, Inc.
1200 Eglinton Avenue East
Suite 200
Don Mills, Ontario M3C 3N1

Macmillan Publishing Company is part of the Maxwell Communication Group of Companies.

First edition
Printed in the United States of America
Printed in Hong Kong by South China Printing Company (1988) Ltd.
10 9 8 7 6 5 4 3 2 1
The text of this book is set in Primer

Sufrin, Mark.
Stephen Crane/by Mark Sufrin.
p   m.
Summary: A biography of the American writer who, despite an untimely death at twenty-eight, secured a place in literary history for his originality, range and complexity.
ISBN 0-689-31669-0
1. Crane, Stephen. 1871-1900—Biography—Juvenile literature. 2. Authors, American—19th century—Biography—Juvenile literature. [1. Crane, Stephen, 1871-1900. 2. Authors, American.] I. Title
PS1449.C85Z94   1992
813'.4—dc20
91-47896

[B]

One

The young man walked quickly toward the glow of gas-light and turned into the Bowery. The noise and colorful crowds, the threatening toughs lurking in dark alleys, and the blaze of lights from saloons and dance halls still astonished him. He thought the notorious street was the most interesting in New York, and later said it gave him his "artistic education." In 1892, the Bowery was the tawdry, dangerous downtown section that offered every forbidden pleasure. Young Stephen Crane felt as if he had suddenly come upon the lost city of his obsessions. Even as a student at Syracuse University, a classmate said, "he liked to talk to shambling figures on slum streets, and his love for adventure constantly kept him in the poolrooms, saloons, red light district, and police station." An artist friend of Crane's said, "Stevie actually found relief in the company of bums and prosti-tutes . . . any kind of lowlife."

Stephen Crane was that classic American figure—the minister's son who rebelled against his father's puritanical vision of life. Reformers called the Bowery "a hotbed of knavery, debauchery, and bestiality." But to Crane it was "real life," and he gloried in it. He hated the "nicely laundered" lives of his family and the "best people" in his hometown, and often went out of his way to shock them. He shunned the dinner table at his brothers' houses because he couldn't tolerate the small talk. His niece, Helen Crane, understood him and once said, "He was the kind of adolescent who would get a thrill out of being shot at sunrise." From his early teens, he smoked, cursed, drank beer, played poker and pool—certain signs of wickedness in that genteel, pious age. Ambitious to be a writer, he left college, sure it had very little to do with the kind of writer he wanted to be.

Standing in the glare of a gas lamp, he hardly seemed the romantic figure of the young, aspiring artist, a turn-of-the-century decadent. Short and slight, he had a sallow complexion accented by the yellowish light, a scraggly mustache, intent blue-gray eyes, and an ironic smile. He slouched in a long, threadbare overcoat that came down to his scuffed shoes, and he had a battered felt hat pushed back on his head.

He loved the Bowery's worldly swagger but never underestimated its menace and vice. It was the place where famed songwriter Stephen Foster had died drunk in a flophouse doorway, and countless men and women had ended in shame and ruin. There was every lurid pleasure and service in its short stretch of fourteen streets: eighty-two saloons, brothels, opium dens, dance halls, cheap vaudeville and melodrama, dime museums, shooting galleries, clip joints, fortune-tellers, tattoo parlors, thieves' markets, pawnbrokers, and barbershops where men read the *Police Gazette* for news of boxing, horse racing, crime, and show business. It would be the inspiration for Crane's first book.

Young men called "bowery boys" stood on the corners. They had mustaches dyed black, wore perfume, and oiled their hair. Their costume was a high silk hat, tight pants, pointed boots, and a black silk scarf under the collar of a flannel shirt. Crane described them "dreaming bloodred dreams when pretty women passed, and threatening mankind at the intersection of streets." He saw sailors wreck a dance hall in a fight over a woman. Walking past a saloon's swinging doors, he was hit by a flying bottle and got a black eye, but continued his exploration.

Everywhere was a swirl of humanity—stumbling drunks, ham actors, flashy con men, sharp-faced jockeys, painted and gaudily dressed prostitutes, immigrants speaking in strange tongues, and the eager tourists lusting for thrills. The fame of the Bowery had spread across the country, and Crane heard the accents of the South and Midwest as middle-aged men tagged after their boy guides. Scarcely older than twelve, most of the boys spent their dollar fees in the saloons that sold them ten-cent pint bottles of whiskey.

There were five-cent flophouses, others where for fifteen cents a man could get a meal of meat and potatoes.

A sign proclaimed LODGINGS FOR MEN ONLY/NICE ROOMS, TWENTY-FIVE CENTS.

A cold rain dripped through the elevated railroad that ran along the Bowery. Horse-drawn carriages rolled up and down the cobbled streets. Gaslight flickered and the sidewalks glistened. Crane saw Steve Brodie glad-handing patrons in his saloon and wondered if he had really jumped off the Brooklyn Bridge six years before. He took careful note of the types in the Atlantic Gardens and Ahearn's saloon. Down an alley, he saw an infamous homosexual brothel hidden by shadows and dark purple curtains on the windows. A rich-looking couple came out of a side-street opium den. Two rivers of people swarmed along the sidewalks. A red streetcar, big and shining with brass, clattered north. Overhead a train came to a stop with grinding wheels.

At Chatham Square, the Bowery's southern boundary, Crane saw aimless men hanging around the elevated station stairs, "standing patiently, like chickens in a storm," he wrote. The rain stopped and he left the Bowery, walking southeast as the Brooklyn Bridge loomed. Now the streets became dark and foul smelling. The old wooden houses and tenements seemed to creak with the weight of humanity. Wet clothes lay on the fire escapes, and doorways were cluttered with buckets, brooms, rags, and bottles. Garbage was strewn along the streets. It was late and dark and cold, but children played or fought in filthy puddles, or sat in the gutter in the way of vehicles. Women with ratty hair and in dirty clothes gossiped while leaning on railings, or screamed in quarrels. Withered old men sat smoking pipes in obscure corners, and the sour smells of cooking wafted to the street.

No nineteenth-century American writer knew New York's demimonde and slums more intimately than Crane. It was out of such unlikely material—rarely used before, and never with his artistry and eye—that he fashioned his first novel, *Maggie: A Girl of the Streets*. It was the story of how environment shaped the life of a girl who "blossomed in a mud puddle," had romantic dreams, was cast out by lover and family, became a prostitute, and killed herself. *Maggie* was the work of a young man who early on understood how an individual could be crushed by society. But it was less documentary than impressionistic nightmare. It had none of the reformer's insistence on economic and sociological factors. Crane was writing about a girl who understood nothing of herself and the world.

He was among the first writers to rebel against the genteel tradition, with its false romanticism and repression. The popular books were historical romances like *When Knighthood Was in Flower*, *Graustark*, and *The Princess Aline*. They were full of flowery and stilted language, sentiment, derring-do, and happy endings. But Crane and some of his contemporaries were learning to mistrust what society taught and accepted. "Let a thing become a tradition and it becomes half a lie," was his blunt conclusion. In his best books, in a crisp style, Crane made his readers face the truth about slum life, war, and the destructive tensions of love and family life. His superb short stories told of the beauty and security of the

American small town—but also of its terror, boredom, and vulnerability. He had an instinctive understanding of American manners and character, its popular memory and legends. He was bitingly original, the first great modern writer. He used everyday, even obscene, speech, popular songs, bawdy ballads, street expressions, popular religion, and sportswriter's jargon. In *Maggie*, a male character tries to express the beauty of the moon—"Deh moon sure looks like hell, don' it?" he says. C. K. Linson, Crane's artist friend, said that the author "had a knack of speaking to cutthroats, preachers, cowboys, soldiers, and business men in their own language. He knew how Americans talked and bagged his game."

Stephen Crane took the 1890s by storm, the "genius boy" of his time. He burst forth young, yet fully grown, seeming to owe no allegiance to any tradition. No one in America had written like him before. He cut through the problems of American society not by large-scale panoramas but by dealing with people's nerve ends. He saw clearly the spreading vulgarity and sordidness of post–Civil War life. The decade of the nineties marked a dividing line between the older, isolated, rural America, and the new urban society. He wrote in a time of middle-class optimism, the growth of big business, and old maxims that dictated "proper" behavior. His world, however, was unsettled, changing, difficult to understand. His characters have a psychological isolation more common to today's world than to the late nineteenth century.

His ability to portray tragedy with understated emotion foreshadowed that of Ernest Hemingway and other twentieth-century writers. Like Hemingway, Crane, throughout his career, seemed suicidally haunted in his far-ranging quests to experience war. It was Crane who established the code of experience that Hemingway later perfected. For Crane it became a stern literary creed: "A man is born into the world with his own pair of eyes, and he is not responsible for his vision—he is merely responsible for his quality of personal honesty." In Hemingway's *The Green Hills of Africa*, published in 1935, a man asks him about the good American writers.

"The good American writers," replied Hemingway, "are Henry James, Stephen Crane, and Mark Twain. That's not the order they're grouped in. There is no order for good writers." Asked what happened to Crane, he said, "He died. That's simple. He was dying from the start."

The critic Alfred Kazin in *On Native Grounds*, an interpretation of American literature, wrote:

Stephen Crane had a ruthless literary courage possible only to those who are afraid. Life tossed him up and down like a cork. To his last days—before dying at twenty-eight—he was tormented by disease and insecurity, greedy friends and witnesses to his genius who thought him a strangely convivial freak. He was wounded by stupid editors, shallow critics, and a doltish public. . . . He was the first great pyrotechnician of the novel, and probably wrote more trash than any other serious novelist of his time. . . . There is a sense of wasted talent. He was the first great tragic figure in the modern American generation.

Crane began by forcing the literary establishment and readers to accept new forms. He ended by writing a pot-boiler novel to try and pay his debts—so that his exhausted imagination could breathe again. Yet, it seems, it wasn't frustration that wore him out, but his own weariness of life. His gift was a furious one, but he repeated himself so joylessly that in the end it seemed self-mockery.

The story of his life leads from his earliest days in a Methodist parsonage to the resort beaches of Asbury Park, New Jersey, into the infamous Bowery and foul slums of New York, through the rugged country of the West and Mexico, and to the battlefields of Greece and Cuba. His imagination transformed those experiences into art. It is an art that expresses a compelling vision of life and marks Crane unmistakably as a major force in modern literature.

TWO

In the early morning of November 1, 1871, Mrs. Mary Crane gave birth to her fourteenth child. Now forty-five, she had lost the last five children in infancy. The father, Reverend Jonathan Townley Crane, pastor of the Central Methodist Church of Newark, New Jersey, noted in his journal:

> Our fourteenth child was born today. We shall call him Stephen Crane for his ancestor who signed the Declaration of Independence.

The minister was mistaken. The ancestor served with the Continental Congress but left Philadelphia a week before the signing. The Cranes, however, were deeply rooted in the nation's history. Cranes were in the first group of colonists that landed at Massachusetts Bay in 1620. They founded New Haven, Connecticut, and Newark, Elizabethtown, and Montclair (once called Crane-town) in New Jersey.

Cranes had served in all the country's wars, and Stephen grew up proud of his military forebears. They were army officers or naval commanders in the French and Indian War, the revolutionary war, the War of 1812, action against the Barbary pirates in 1815, the Mexican War, and the tragic Civil War that ended only six years before his birth. The illustrious family made a deep impression on him and helped shape his imagination. They represented the true aristocracy, people who stand firmly to their duty, regardless of risk. "I swear by the real aristocrat," he wrote. "The man whose forefathers were men of courage, sympathy and wisdom is one who will stand the strain. He is like a thoroughbred horse. His nerves may be high, but in the crisis he becomes the most reliable and enduring of men." That idea would surface again and again in Crane's writings.

The Methodist parsonage where Stephen was born was a small redbrick house on a fashionable street. His father, fifty-two, was busy writing books on Methodist doctrine and codes of conduct. He was against dancing, smoking, card playing, drinking, singing popular songs, and reading popular novels. The minister also spent much time as presiding elder of sixteen Methodist churches in Newark. Stephen remembered his bearded, spectacled father as "simple and good, but I often think he didn't know much of anything about humanity."

His mother came from a long line of Methodist preachers. She was involved with temperance and social

Stephen Crane at age two, 1873
George Arents Research Library,
Syracuse University

reform movements, wrote religious articles for New
York newspapers, and was in demand as a speaker. In-
flexible in her religion, she was a homely, fragile-
looking woman of uncommon will and determination.
Stephen was astonished that "such an intellectual
woman would have wrapped herself so completely in the
vacuous, futile, psalm-singing that passed for worship in
those days."

When he was born, Stephen's nearest sibling was his

brother Luther, aged eight. The oldest brother was George, twenty-one, and the oldest Crane child was sister Mary Helen, twenty-two. Two brothers, William, then seventeen, and Townley, nineteen, would play important roles in Stephen's future. His middle-aged parents were too busy in the causes of Christ and Methodism to nurture their unexpected child, and his care was given to sister Agnes, then fifteen. She was the most important influence of his early years. She called herself "my mother's ugly duckling," but she was literary and gifted—wanted "first to be a Christian lady, then a writer"—and she lavished attention on her small brother. He was a sickly child, with constant colds, and she nursed him, directed his reading, and a little later encouraged his first efforts to write stories and poems.

Because of their life in the church, Stephen's parents were always on the move. In 1874 they were in Bloomington, New Jersey, on the Raritan River, where Stephen almost drowned after wading out too far. Two years later they moved to Paterson, New Jersey, when Reverend Crane became pastor of the Cross Street Church. Two years after that the family was again transferred, this time to Port Jervis, New York, a typical rural village of that era of American innocence. Situated in the hills of southwestern New York, the town and countryside would figure large in Crane's work. Main Street, which had no stores or commercial buildings, curved around broad-porched houses and spreading lawns past the elder Crane's church. In the valleys below there were resort hotels. To the north, stretching toward the Catskill

Stephen Crane at age five, 1876
Clifton Waller Barrett Collection,
Alderman Library, University of Virginia

Mountains, was the wilderness of Sullivan County, which Crane came to know as a camper, hunter, and fisherman. Port Jervis became the model for the village in his novel, *The Third Violet*, and the fictional town of "Whilomville" in the tales of childhood in *Whilomville Stories*. The rocky, deep-wooded wilderness was also the setting for the *Sullivan County Sketches*.

Because he was a delicate child, Stephen didn't start formal school until he was eight. But he had had a head start because his sister had taught him science, arithmetic, nature lore, and literature. "They tell me I got through two grades in six weeks," he said later, "which sounds like the lie of a fond mother at a tea party, but I do remember that I got ahead very fast and that Father was very pleased with me."

The placid life of the parsonage was suddenly shattered when Reverend Crane died of a heart attack on February 16, 1880. The house was full of people for the funeral. It was all ghastly to the thin, small boy—the whispering, the hymn singing by country women, the heavy odors and darkness, his tall brothers dressed in black. He was terrified when his hand brushed a cold, silver handle on the coffin. Twenty years later, the day was still vivid to him:

> We tell kids that heaven is just across the gaping grave and all that bosh, and then we scare them to glue with flowers and white sheets and hymns. We ought to be crucified for it! . . . I have forgotten nothing about that day, not a damned iota, not a shred.

Though he rebelled against everything his father stood for, Crane always spoke admiringly of him: "Once, Will gave me a toy gun and I tried to shoot a cow with it. It upset Father terribly. He loved all kinds of animals, and never drove a horse faster than two yards an hour even if some Christian was dying somewhere."

He began to devour paperback dime novels in secret—*Terror of the Sagebrush, Black Dick of the Pony Express*—and played Wild West with other boys. A sister-in-law remembered him as "a loveable boy, full of life and animal spirits." He began to show an interest in the military and war, and loved to read *Harper's Illustrated History of the Rebellion.* Gathering buttons from his mother and sisters, he marched them in little regiments, re-creating great battles of history, particularly the Civil War. Throughout his life he would imagine, chase, report, fictionalize, and remember war.

In the first uncertain months after his father's death, the family lived in a boardinghouse in Roseville, near Newark. Stephen became dangerously sick with scarlet fever, and when he recovered his mother took him back to the healthier climate of Port Jervis. Agnes began teaching at a town school, and brother William set up a law practice there. In the spring of 1883, Mrs. Crane moved to Asbury Park, a vacation town on the New Jersey shore. It was only a mile north of Ocean Grove, the Methodist center where a great religious encampment was held every summer. "After my father died, my mother lived only for religion," Stephen said. His eccentric brother

Crane's mother, Mary Helen Peck Crane, 1889
George Arents Research Library,
Syracuse University

Townley was a reporter for the *Newark Advertiser* and during the summer operated a news agency in Asbury Park. He supplied short items to the *New York Tribune* and Associated Press about the resort hotels, Ocean Grove religious conferences, and concerts and lectures in nearby Avon-by-the-Sea. Agnes, unhappy in Port Jervis, took a teaching job in the Asbury Park school where Stephen was a pupil and sister Mary an art instructor.

Asbury Park meant freedom for Stephen, "a pale-faced, blond-headed, hungry-looking boy," as a boyhood friend remembered him. He roamed the beaches, hung around Townley's agency and the big hotels, and played baseball and football with ferocious spirit. In June 1884 Stephen, now twelve, suffered "one of the greatest losses of my life." Agnes, only twenty-eight, died of spinal meningitis, and the boy grieved over his dearest friend. To cheer him up, Townley gave him a retired circus pony, and he took long rides exploring the countryside. Something of a daredevil, he often plunged into the surf while riding bareback, clinging to the pony's mane. Once he rode past the camp of a road construction crew and saw a girl stabbed by her lover. He galloped home, sweating with fear and confusion at the sight of irrational violence, but said nothing about it for a long time.

After Agnes died, he came under the more worldly influence of his brothers. They had long rejected their parents' strict religion and wanted Stephen to do the same.

"William tried to argue with Mother about religion, but he always gave up," Stephen later recalled. "You could just as well argue with a wave. I used to like church and prayer meeting when I was a kid, but that cooled off and when I was thirteen or about that, my brother Will told me not to believe in Hell after my uncle had been boring me about the Lake of Fire and the rest of those sideshows."

His mother worried that he was giving up belief in eternal damnation and salvation. "Stevie is like the wind in Scripture," she told a friend. "He bloweth where he listeth." But he was already flouting the Methodist and temperance union rules.

"Once when I was fourteen, an organ grinder on the beach gave me a nice long drink out of a nice red bottle for picking up his hat. I felt ecstatic walking home and then I was an Emperor and some Rajahs at the same time. I'd been sulky all morning, but now I was perfectly willing to go to a prayer meeting and Mother was tickled to death. And mind you, all because this nefarious Florentine gave me a red drink out of a bottle. I have frequently wondered how much mothers ever know about their sons, after all. I was quietly drunk."

The passage indicates a sense of guilt and alienation, and Crane drew on it for his novel *George's Mother*. It dramatized the disastrous consequences of a willful young man's alcoholic revolt against his religious mother.

During summers he was the outstanding catcher and youngest member of the Asbury Park baseball team. He wrote to a friend that he wanted to be a professional baseball player. "But ma says it's not a serious occupation and Will says I have to go to college first." He already had the urge to write and between games of a double-header composed an essay that won a twenty-five-cent prize. A boy of fourteen who could use words like "irascible, pyrotechnic, partiality" in an essay written in fifteen minutes was not like other American boys. He early showed a passion for outlandish words and invented one: *higgle*—to behave in the manner of a schoolteacher. At fourteen he wrote a story, "Uncle Jake and the Bell-Handle," which is his earliest known manuscript. It is about an old farmer who visits the city, sees a bell-handle, doesn't understand its use, but pulls it and summons fire engines.

He was fast becoming his own person: small, but wiry and athletic; peering warily at the world with the large, steady blue-gray eyes; indifferent to school, but with a keen sense that the world adults described and prized was different from the one he observed. His intuition told him that whatever was accepted was suspect—that there was an inside story behind every public history.

In September 1885, two months shy of his fourteenth birthday, his mother sent him to Pennington, a Methodist seminary founded in New Jersey by his father. She thought the school would teach him discipline and in some way place him once more under his father's influence. There were services twice daily in the school chapel, services Sunday morning in one of the village's two churches, Bible classes Sunday afternoon in the chapel, and general prayer meetings Wednesday evenings. For Stephen it was a disagreeably dramatic contrast to the years of roaming free in Asbury Park, but he stuck it out for two and a half years.

He then persuaded his mother to send him to Claverack College and Hudson Military Institute, a semimilitary, coeducational school in New York. Claverack was founded by Methodists, but by the time Stephen arrived, it had all but been absorbed by the undistinguished military school. Most of the students were rebellious or backward boys, and the school's standards and discipline had sharply declined. Harvey Wickham, a Crane classmate, wrote in a 1926 magazine article: "Boys and girls roamed as if in a terrestrial paradise like packs of wolves out of bounds, out of hours and very much out of hand."

For Crane it was a "bully time, simply pie." He was popular and quickly became a leader with the boys and a pest to the faculty. "I never learned anything there. American private schools are not as bad as our public schools, perhaps, but there is no great difference. . . . But heaven was sunny blue and no rain fell on the diamond when I played baseball. I was very happy there." He had always caught pitches barehanded, but now he was playing with bigger, more powerful young men, and late in the season he started wearing a buckskin glove. In those days each player wore whatever uniform he wanted. "The diamond presented an appearance of Joseph in the Bible days with his coat of many colors."

He was a poor student in science and mathematics—when he chose to attend classes—but far more advanced in literature and history because of Agnes's teaching. Once he called Tennyson's poetry "swill" and got into a fistfight and lost a tooth. As punishment he had to memorize and recite the poet's "Charge of the Light Brigade," an agony he used in one of the *Whilomville* stories. Abram Travis, another classmate, remembered Crane as a voracious reader of nineteenth-century English writers and Roman and Greek classics. But then and in later life he was never "literary" or bookish.

He was elected captain of the baseball team but declined in favor of another player he felt deserved the honor. He became adjutant of the corps of cadets and first lieutenant of crack C company, which won the coveted Washington's Birthday drill prize. He was a talented drillmaster but a martinet. Wickham said, "He had enough of the true officer in him to have a henlike attitude toward the rank and file. No, Stevie was not tender of other people's feelings."

He was first infatuated with a redheaded student named Harriet Mattison. Then he was in rapture about another redhead, Jenny Pierce, whom he "loved madly, and who could make my life miserable with only half an effort." Next came a tall, dark girl and then a blonde.

A photograph of Stephen Crane in his school uniform shows a pleasant-looking youth with a well-shaped head, prominent nose, full mouth, and large, expressive eyes. His hair is fashionably parted on one side and trimmed in a kind of half bang slanting across his forehead. He seems the correct middle-class cadet. But he was notoriously sloppy, wearing baggy pants and a torn, dirty

Stephen Crane as a lieutenant in the Hudson Military Institute cadet corps, 1889

Clifton Waller Barrett Collection,
Alderman Library, University of Virginia

sweater out of uniform, and unconventional in his ways and speech. To boys who never penetrated his seeming aloofness, he seemed arrogant. He didn't seem to give a damn if anyone liked him or not, and in Wickham's words, "enjoyed a certain reputation for 'villainy.' "

There were contradictions in his behavior. He played the tough rebel, but he was a close friend of the richest boy in school and considered himself an authentic aristocrat. He could curse a man blue on the drill field but hated the cadets' cruel and humiliating practical jokes. He affected slangy, low-class speech but wrote excellent stories and articles for the school magazine. In bull sessions he railed against religion, yet sang in the choir. For all his bold talk, he was something of a prude, refusing to hang around the shoemaker who told dirty stories. He avoided a pie shop where local Don Juans sat on dark stairs with certain girls. Wickham, who seemed fascinated by Crane, said, "He seldom went into Hudson, our neighboring and deliciously wicked city, where according to rumor, initiation was to be had into the ultimate mysteries of life." Wickham once also heard him say to a reputed seducer, "I hear you're bad—I hear you're damned bad." His instinct for rebellion, his "bad boy" behavior, clashed dramatically with the ethical values of his Methodist heritage, for all his contempt of religion. There was an unresolved tension in him between piety and sinfulness, authority and rebellion.

The only faculty member he respected was his history teacher, Reverend General John Bullock Van Petten, a veteran of the Civil War. The old man personified both the true Christian and brave soldier, the two strands of Crane's heritage. Flushed with excitement, the general often told of his experiences, especially the terrible Battle of Antietam. The school had revived Stephen's interest in the military, and he thought he would become a professional soldier. He was also inspired by brother William, a student of the battles of Chancellorsville and Gettysburg. In *The Red Badge of Courage*, Crane's masterpiece, the plank road and pontoon identified Chancellorsville. But it was General Van Petten's account of the rout at Antietam that suggested the panicky flight from combat of Henry Fleming, the book's protagonist. In the book Claverack and Hudson became the seminary where Henry Fleming "bid farewell to many schoolmates. . . . A certain light-haired girl made vivacious fun at his martial spirit, but there was another and darker girl whom he had gazed at steadfastly, and he thought she grew demure and sad at sight of his blue and brass."

Summers he worked for Townley, gathering news for his brother's column in the Sunday *New York Tribune*. Asbury Park was an important influence in Crane's view of the world. He was, supremely, an observer, and the town taught him the double standards of morality. Named for Francis Asbury, founder of the Methodist church in America, it was becoming the typical resort. He saw adultery, prostitution, heavy drinking, and gambling, the abuse of poorly paid employees by "stern proper Christians," the gaudy amusement park and rides with their incessant steam-organ music, street vendors hawking cheap novelties, and "young people finding a sordid sanctuary under the boardwalk."

Young Crane, however, gloried in the hypocrisy, sin, and tinsel. He saw it as confirmation of his cold, unsentimental eye, and proof against his parents' version of religion. He took up with a sporting crowd and learned to live in the world of men. Friends remember him as "a good companion and a young man who liked fun and danger." One recalled his "keen sense of the dramatic, and his amused, satirical grin. His keen mind instantly caught the absurd, bizarre or ridiculous aspect of any incident. . . ."

Crane didn't graduate from Claverack. Brother Will apparently persuaded him to give up his plan for an army career. Will said that since the family owned stock in a Pennsylvania coal mine, a more practical profession would be mining engineering. In the fall of 1890, Stephen became a student at Lafayette College in Easton, Pennsylvania, a school that specialized in engineering. For someone of Crane's gifts, interests, and temperament, it was the worst choice. In those years Lafayette's curriculum was narrow and conservative, and mining engineering was notoriously the least inspiring. Students wrote papers only in their specialized fields and only "in the words and phrases current among experts." Instruction—even the sciences—was keyed to religious doctrine.

Crane enrolled in courses in the poet John Milton, the Bible, algebra, geometry, drawing, chemistry, and

French but was rarely in class. Baseball was long months away, but he played pickup intramural games nearly every day. He boxed a little and could often be found drinking beer in a poolroom, talking literature while lining up a shot. He thought Leo Tolstoy was the world's greatest writer, wasn't too enthusiastic about Gustave Flaubert, and hated Robert Louis Stevenson. He said one of Henry James's books was a bore, and though they later became good friends, Crane never liked his work much.

He had pledged the Delta Upsilon fraternity, and in the first weeks he expected a visit from the hazing squad. One night he suddenly heard loud knocking at his dormitory door. He didn't answer, hoping they'd think he was out. The fraternity boys broke the door down, rushed in, and lit a lamp. "Crane looked ghastly in the lamplight and extremely nervous as he stood in a grotesque nightgown in a corner with a loaded revolver in his hand," said one of the hazers. "There was no time to escape what might have proved a real tragedy until Crane unexpectedly lowered the revolver and motioned to us to get out." There was no further thought of hazing him, and he was accepted into the fraternity. He had bought the revolver for five dollars from a westerner stranded in Asbury Park.

Crane's stay at Lafayette contributed something to *Red Badge*. There was annual combat between freshmen and sophomores to capture the others' flag. Crane, fighting furiously and directing classmates, seized the sophomore banner just as an upper classman smashed him in the face. He sent a piece torn from the banner to a Claverack friend: "It doesn't look like much does it? But just remember I got a black and blue nose, a painful shin, skin torn off my hands, and a lame shoulder in the fight." The incident became the dramatic moment in *Red Badge* when a battle flag is wrenched from the hands of a Confederate soldier.

At the end of his first semester, Crane received grades in only four of his seven courses, and two were failing marks. The other three weren't graded because he never attended the classes. After the Christmas holiday, he returned to Lafayette but just to pack, saying only that he had to leave school because of some family trouble. The truth was that he had flunked out but intended to leave, anyway. "I went to Lafayette College but didn't graduate. I found mining engineering not at all to my taste. I preferred baseball."

Still hopeful that a Methodist education would benefit her drifting and sometimes wayward son, Mrs. Crane shipped him off to Syracuse University. His great-uncle, Bishop Jessie Peck, was one of the founders of the school. Townley got him a job as Syracuse correspondent for the *New York Tribune*. That, and the fact that the university was a baseball power, made him look forward to another brush with higher education. His entrance into the city confirmed his optimism. As the train rolled along Railroad Street, he saw painted women peering from the windows or porches of the eighteen "parlor houses" along the New York Central tracks. Syracuse was a big city with seedy areas to explore and, he later learned, other houses of prostitution downtown near the best hotels. He wrote his Claverack friends, "There are some damn pretty girls at school, praise be to God. This is a dandy city and I expect to see some fun here."

He transferred his Delta Upsilon membership from Lafayette and, according to his mother's plan, stayed with his great-aunt, the bishop's widow. The elderly Mrs. Peck, however, was unhappy with his ideas about life and living, and he moved briefly to a cheap boarding-house. He then shared a room in the fraternity house, littering it with tobacco cans and pipes, books and paper and news clippings, athletic uniforms and equipment, signs and drawings. Slow and deliberate in his move-ments, often moody, he would on other occasions talk with great wit and originality in a soft, lazy drawl. Class-mates remembered his kindness and consideration, with, one said, "great solicitude for the comfort and welfare of other people of narrow means." Like his father, he was passionately fond of animals and said he automatically trusted anyone who showed affection for dogs and horses.

He was, predictably, indifferent to formal education. After a talk with Crane, a professor said, "We look upon him as an exceedingly bright young man, of large ca-pacity, but he will not be cramped following a course of study he does not care for." He and his friends defied "the grim Methodist environment" by doing everything forbidden, including occasional sorties into the red-light district, and he haunted the slums and police court. He had fierce contempt for almost all the faculty. A professor

Crane (seated right) *with friends at Syracuse University, 1891*
Clifton Waller Barrett Collection,
Alderman Library, University of Virginia

scolded him for offering an unorthodox idea and reminded him of St. Paul's position on the question. "I know what St. Paul said," he replied, "but I disagree with St. Paul." He also had little respect for religious reformers, and when Frances Willard, the famous temperance leader and reformer, visited the university, Crane refused to hear her. "She's a fool. One of those wonderful people who can tell right from wrong for everybody from the polar cap to the equator. Perhaps it never struck her that people differ from her. I have loved myself passionately now and then, but Miss Willard's affair with Miss Willard should be stopped by the police."

Baseball practice started, and Crane spent more time on the field than in the classroom. His reputation had preceded him. The *Syracusan*, the school paper, noted that "Crane, the old catcher of the Lafayette College team, has entered the University and will make a good addition to the team." Manning French was the star pitcher, and more than forty years later he recalled Crane in an alumni publication:

I had a very good fast ball, but Stephen refused to wear the big catcher's mitt and preferred the less awkward padded finger glove. Everytime I threw the fast ball, he caught it but was lifted off his feet backwards. He never complained. He had the habit of striking his fist three or four times into the glove to express his approval of a "strike" when missed by a batter. When we succeeded in striking out our man, an expression of fiendish glee would light up

Crane in Syracuse University baseball uniform, spring 1891
George Arents Research Library,
Syracuse University

his face, and he always expressed his appreciation when our opponents were retired to end an inning. He was quick and excitable on the diamond, always in motion, talkative and wantonly profane. He could be sarcastic with teammates who made poor plays, but generous with praise when they made good ones. He was a fast baserunner, had a weak throwing arm, and was a good but not hard hitter.

Stephen began to write seriously. He did pieces for the *New York Tribune* and had a short story published in the university literary magazine. The most important thing he did at Syracuse was to write the story of a prostitute—a nineteen-year-old—mining material for a book that would spur the beginning of modern American literature. Friends who read it thought later it might have been a first draft of *Maggie: A Girl of the Streets*, but based on observations in Syracuse's tenement district. *Maggie*, however, was probably written soon after when Crane began to explore the Bowery and slums of lower Manhattan.

He flunked algebra, chemistry, physics, education, and German but received an *A* in English literature. The dean suggested that he'd be happier elsewhere, but Crane had no intention of attending another school.

I did little work at Syracuse, but confined my abilities, such as they were, to the diamond. Not that I disliked books, but the cut and dried curriculum of the college did not appeal to me. Humanity was a much more interesting study. When I ought to have been at recitations, I was studying faces on the streets, and when I ought to have been studying my next day's lessons, I was watching the trains roll in and out of the station.

So, you see, I had, first of all, to recover from college. I had to build up, so to speak.

$\mathcal{T}$hree

Crane spent the summer of 1891 in Asbury Park—"that most American of towns"—working as a full-time reporter for Townley's news agency. His brother also turned over most of the *Tribune* column work to him. Crane combed that stretch of the Jersey shore to pick up news and gossip for human-interest items. In his spare time he played baseball, lounged on the beach, practiced target shooting with his revolver, and occasionally went into New York City.

Ralph Paine, a friend, thought it remarkable that "a youth with the soul of a poet and a psychologist should find even in that futile, trivial environment of Asbury Park in midsummer encouragement for his literary ambitions." But the resort was a lively scene, the best kind of education for a young writer with Crane's gift of observation and sense of irony—the contrast between what is expected or seems to happen and what actually occurs.

Crane saw the contradictions in the free-spending vacationers in the gingerbread hotels, who pursued religion in Ocean Grove and culture and self-improvement in Avon-by-the-Sea. He now began to look upon this world as a potential literary scene, because those communities were a neat microcosm of America. Before him lay all the conflicts in the nation's social, cultural, and religious life.

Asbury Park was created for "wholesome amusement." It attracted prosperous families to the comforts of the hotels, and the pleasures of the beach, boardwalk, amusement park, and music hall. Crane, however, was drawn to the hidden life of sex, gambling, and boozing behind the innocent summer fun. He also noted the growing taste for more worldly, daring amusement among the young, which his mother lamented "keeps them from the house of God." He wrote about the hypocrisy—that split between self-centered pleasure and moral discipline—with satire and irony.

In a seemingly innocent article for the *Tribune*, he wrote about the shallow, selfish "summer girl" and her dandified suitor, "a golden boy," as types of mindless vanity. Exquisitely gowned, the summer girl poses against the backdrop of the somber ocean, chewing gum slowly in time with the rolling surf. The scene shows Crane's sense of people's alienation from nature, one of his major themes. In another piece, he talks about poker players in Asbury Park rattling their fifty-dollar chips as they listen to far-off sounds from Ocean Grove of "5,000 throats singing the doxology," the praise of God.

Crane lived in this house in Asbury Park, New Jersey.

One of the most important events in Crane's life happened on a late August day that summer. He went to Avon-by-the-Sea to cover a lecture by Hamlin Garland, a young radical writer and critic from Boston. That day Garland was lecturing on William Dean Howells, an older, respected novelist, critic, and editor of the *Atlantic Monthly*. After Garland read Crane's review in the *Tribune*, he asked to see him. When Crane appeared—"a reticent young fellow with a big German pipe in his mouth, small and sallow and inclined to stoop"—they talked mostly baseball. Over the next few days they talked some about writing, but usually Garland pitched to Crane on the beach, and they theorized about pitching "inshoots" and "outdrops" to confound a batter. Garland called him "an excellent catcher of curve balls." When he left for Boston he never expected to see Crane again.

To Crane, the intense, self-assured Garland was an admirable example of the new radical writer. He became famous with a collection of realistic stories about life on the great western prairie and was a contributor to the influential *Harper's Weekly* magazine. Garland was never more than a mediocre writer, but his theory of what literature should be impressed Crane. Garland believed that evolution ensured a constant unfolding of new and better forms in society and the arts, as well as in nature. He wanted new styles, new subjects, new forms. The only true subject, Garland declared, was contemporary American life—the immense variety of color and movement in the broad national scene, in the big city, the slums, the remote mountains and prairies.

Another important event that summer would prove shattering to Crane. He fell in love with a young singer named Helen Trent. The tall, dark young woman was staying at a resort hotel before sailing for London to marry an English doctor. Crane didn't know about the impending marriage and followed her to New York in September. She was packing when her servant announced his arrival, and he was ushered into the ornate drawing room of her guardian's Greenwich Village house.

Unusual for him, he was well dressed and barbered but later felt he was shy and dull that day. He told her of his first adventures in the Bowery and tenement districts, his ambition to write a book about that life one day. He talked about Hamlin Garland, who he said "looked like a nice Jesus Christ," and expressed the opinion that "Christianity is mildewed." Helen and her ardent young swain quarreled about the Bowery, which she thought "a terrible place." Crane left in anger but wrote her a remorseful, twelve-page letter on Fifth Avenue Hotel stationery.

Crane liked to shock her with his literary opinions, his idea that "a Negro man can be considered handsome without the classic profile," or that Buddhism was far more interesting than the "mean, punishing, American religions." He said he was going back to the Bowery and the slums again and again, and she forbade him. He said that nobody had written a book about that kind of life, and—*couldn't she see?*—he had to learn how these people lived and talked and thought. They quarreled again and he left, but he mailed her a note just before he took the ferry to New Jersey: "I shall come back tomorrow and we can start all over again."

Mostly she played the piano and sang for him. He lit her cigarettes while voicing disapproval of a woman's smoking. One evening she showed him her guardian's boudoir, all florid velvet and enamel, and he slyly remarked, "When will the stagehands take it away?" One day she refused to see him and he wrote her: "Your window was lighted all last night, but they said you were not in. I stood and looked at your window until a policeman came and made me go away. But I came back and looked until my head was a sponge of lights. Please do not treat me like this."

There was an ironic and poignant epilogue to that first great love of his life. Helen Trent saw Crane only once more, but he was unaware of her. He had, perhaps, a sort of revenge for being the callow, spurned lover. A few months before his death, he was pointed out to her in a London theater as "the famous Stephen Crane." She recognized him but wondered what he was famous for. Yet she had saved all his notes and letters, and as late as 1923 remembered that she had once sewn a button on his coat and persuaded him to brush his hair.

At this time Crane was living at his brother Edmund's house in Lake View, New Jersey. He wrote some of the Sullivan County sketches there and organized the town's first football team, coaching and playing quarterback. He later claimed that football gave him the sense of rage and conflict he drew on for the battle scenes in *Red Badge*. He made trips to New York to try and get a newspaper job, and made friends with young writers and artists who often put him up when he stayed in the city overnight.

He read Rudyard Kipling's *Light That Failed*, and it made a powerful impression on him. The hero of the novel, Dick Heldar, must have represented all that the twenty-year-old Crane hoped to become. Dick is a realist painter and newspaper artist in sharp revolt against genteel art and all respectability. Professor James Colvert in his *Stephen Crane*, says, "Dick Heldar is a free-living Bohemian who finds 'unvarnished truth' in the violence of slums and battlefields. He chooses to suffer poverty and hardship in the slums because he thinks the 'belly pinch' of hunger will make him a better artist." The novel shimmers with color: "Opal and umber and amber and brick-red sulphur against brown, with a black rock and a decorative frieze of camels against a pure pale turquoise sky." It inspired Crane, reinforced his instinct to use color in his work, and color soon became an integral, stunning element of his style.

After his mother died in December 1891, Crane plunged into the bohemian life of New York, resolved to capture for literature the color and hurly-burly of life in the big city. He tramped the newspaper offices in Park Row for a job but was always turned away. He stayed in cheap hotels and boardinghouses, spending much of his time roaming the streets and tenements around the Bowery. His life was barely better than those he studied. With no regular income, almost starved, and often in desperate circumstances, he wrote a note to a friend: "Please send me $5 by this bearer whose name is only Smith. Am going to Ed's house at Lakeview and need some grub. Otherwise I shall eat the front door, his baby and the cat."

His family nagged him to stop his wanderings in the

slums. His brother Wilbur admired Stephen's command of language, his sense of the absurd and sardonic humor, and enjoyed talking to him. But he felt he was not going to be a success as a newspaperman and suggested another line of work. Whenever the subject came up, Stephen disappeared. Helen Crane, Wilbur's daughter, said:

At a family dinner, Uncle Steve would suddenly interrupt talk about neighbors, sickness, weather, or new hats to ask with a perfectly straight face, "Have any of you ever seen a Chinaman wandering in Mott Street?" He could talk all night with William Dean Howells and Hamlin Garland about the Single Tax, the genius of Tolstoy, or the paintings of Thomas Eakins. But when it came to gossip and inane small talk, he was sunk. He just couldn't stand it and was very unpredictable in what he said.

Despite his contempt for his family, he constantly borrowed money from his brothers and felt guilty until the end of his life. "I was foolishly proud then. I hated to borrow money from my brothers who were not too well off. I borrowed too much which I never paid back. They have never asked me for a cent and that hurts like hellfire."

Back in Asbury Park for the summer of 1892, Crane took over most of the news agency's work because Townley was more interested in drinking and playing poker. Now Crane was even more aware of the literary possibilities of the scene. Developing a bolder and more supple style, he described crowds of preachers, young people, entertainers, and stolid businessmen flowing along the boardwalk and boulevards.

"In the evenings," he wrote, "it is a glare of light and a swirl of gaily attired women and well-dressed men." This world of people "is situated somewhere under the long line of electric lights which dangle over the great cosmopolitan thoroughfare. It is the world of the middle classes. Add but princes and gamblers and it would be what the world calls the world."

In one *Tribune* column, he wrote a portrait of the typical summer visitor, so sharp it would have been valid fifty years later:

> He is a portly man with a gold watch-chain strung across the vest of a business suit, a wife and three children, more or less. He stands in his shoes with American self-reliance and, playing casually with his watch-chain, looks at the world with a clear eye. He submits to the outrageous prices of the resort hotels with a calm indifference. He will pay fancy prices for things with great unconcern. However, deliberately attempt to beat him out of fifteen cents and he will jam his hands in his pockets, spread his legs and wrangle in a loud voice until sundown.

> All day he lies in the sand or sits on a bench, reading papers and smoking cigars, while his blessed babies are throwing sand down his neck and emptying their little pails of sea water in his boots. In the evening he puts on his best and takes his wife and the "girls" down to the boardwalk. He enjoys himself in a very mild way and dribbles out a lot of money under the impression that he is getting away cheaply.

Willis Johnson, a *Tribune* editor vacationing at Asbury Park, learned that Crane had written stories based on his camping and hunting adventures in the country around Port Jervis. He bought five for the paper's Sunday feature page. These Sullivan County sketches were far different from tales of young men hiking and fishing, enjoying the healthy beauty of nature, the usual fare in sportsmen's magazines.

The protagonist of these "little grotesque tales of the woods," as Crane described them, is an anonymous "little man" who wanders the fields and forests with three friends. They challenge what he believes to be the threatening spirit of nature, the sinister power of a strange and hostile world. A cave's "black mouth gaped at him." He is angry when a "mesmeric mountain" seems to glower at him, and he "conquers" it by scrambling furiously to its summit. He cowers in terror at the wailing of a demon in the haunted night and is frozen with fear when a "ghoul" snatches him away from the glowing campfire. The face of "an enraged man" peers over the bushes.

But this evil in nature, as Crane's irony reveals, is an illusion, a creation of the little man's morbid anxieties. The cave's black mouth is nothing more than "a little tilted hole" on a hillside. The awful cry of the demon is only the howling of a dog. The sinister mountain, once climbed, is simply a hill "motionless under his feet." The ghoul is only an ignorant farmer who wants him to add a column of figures. The face of the enraged man is the sun sinking behind the treetops.

One of Crane's Asbury Park columns cast an unrelenting eye on the "summer romance," the dream of so many young vacationers. He wrote of its promise and excitement—and the eventual disillusionment. Allowing for its gentler setting and naive models, it could be contemporary for today.

> The amount of summer girl and golden youth business that goes on around the boardwalk is amazing. A young man comes here, maybe from a distant city. Everything is new to him, and, in consequence, he is a new man. He is not the same steady, sensible lad who bent all winter over the ledger in the city office. There is a little more rose-tint and gilt-edge to him. The young man walks out in his false colors and finds on the beach or boardwalk a summer girl who attracts him. She exactly fits his new environment, a bit of interesting, flashing tinsel who gives the zest of life. The young man has a brief, breathless, unrequited fling—then returns to the ledger as he lays down his coat of strange colors and visions fade.

Crane was having his own summer fling with a married woman named Lily Brandon Munroe. Her geologist husband was away on a research trip, and she was staying with her mother and sister in one of the hotels. She was a lovely, patrician blonde who lived in Washington, D.C., and New York. She and Crane rode the merry-go-round, danced, ate ice cream in the finest place, and took long walks along the boardwalk. He confided to her, said he did not expect to live long, and all he wanted was a few years of happiness. She liked him, found him interesting, but with a troubled spirit. She wasn't happily

Lily Brandon Munroe
Clifton Waller Barrett Collection,
Alderman Library, University of Virginia

married, but he was hardly a man for an adulterous affair if she had such an idea. He was poor and undernourished, smoked too much, and had a hacking cough. She didn't think him handsome, but she was attracted to him and always remembered his remarkable almond-shaped eyes. She was touched by the intensity of his feelings but also thought he was too impractical and visionary.

Before he recovered from his infatuation—"the desperation of proud youth" was his phrase—Crane wrote a story, "The Pace of Youth." It tells with wry and tender irony of a touching courtship set against the great ocean and grand sweep of the night sky. The story clearly draws on his "affair" with Lily Munroe. The very weekend the story appeared in the *New York Press* of January 18, 1895, he was trying to convince her to leave her husband and join him on a romantic trip to the West and Mexico. But after divorcing her husband that same year, she married another man. Only months before she remarried, Crane had written to her:

"Don't forget me, dear, never, never, never. For you are to me the only woman in my life. I am doomed, I suppose, to a lonely existence and futile dreams. It has made me better, it has widened my understanding of people and my sympathy for whatever they endure. And to it I owe whatever I have achieved and the hope of the future. In truth, this change in my life should prove of some value to me, for ye gods, I have paid a price for it."

One day in late August, Crane filed a story with the *Tribune* that abruptly ended his career in Asbury Park. It became known among friends and family as "the parade that made Stevie famous." He was covering the parade of the Junior Order of United American Mechanics, an organization of patriotic workingmen. As the parade started, Crane was leaning in the doorway of a billiard parlor, an unlit cigar clenched in his teeth. He noted with interest the contrast between "these bronzed, slope-shouldered, uncouth and begrimed" men of the working class and the crowd of spectators "composed of summer gowns, lace parasols, tennis trousers, straw hats and indifferent smiles." He went back to the office and wrote a vivid, mocking story about the event.

The "Juniors," he noted, had no proper idea of marching:

> It was probably the most awkward, ungainly, uncut and uncarved procession that ever raised dust on sunbeaten streets. But this rabble of hundreds of marchers, plodding along to the "furious discords" of brass bands, were men of "tan-colored, sunbeaten honesty," unlike the "bona fide Asbury Parker . . . to whom a dollar, when held close to the eye, often shuts out any impression he may have had that other people possess rights. And this crowd of summer idlers found vaguely amusing these "spraddle-legged men . . . whose hands were bent and shoulders stooped from digging and constructing. . . .

Somehow the article slipped by the *Tribune* editors and caused a crisis when it appeared. That summer politicians were busy wooing the labor vote. One of them was Whitelaw Reid, owner of the *Tribune* and a candidate for vice president on the Republican ticket. Editors at rival Democratic papers quickly misrepresented the story—Crane, they said, had insulted American workingmen. Actually Crane had mocked the summer crowd even more, but the story was cited as the *Tribune*'s secret bias against labor. The incident snowballed until everyone believed that the United American Mechanics—an organization dedicated to restricting immigration and cheap labor—had paraded that day for the Republican candidate. The Democratic candidate, Grover Cleveland, was eventually elected president.

The *Asbury Park Journal* reported that the *Tribune*'s regular writer was "engaged elsewhere that day and delegated the task of covering the parade to a young man who had a hankering for razzle-dazzle style, and who has a great future ahead of him if, unlike the good, he fails to die young. He thought it smart to sneer at the United Mechanics for their personal appearance and marching." Whitelaw Reid ordered his editor to print a retraction and fired Townley and Crane. According to a friend, Stephen "wore the saintly smile he always has ready for every disaster." Townley, already notorious as an eccentric and alcoholic, ended his career a broken man.

Stephen returned to Port Jervis and stayed with brother Will, now a well-established lawyer. He did a short spell as a reporter on the *Newark Morning Times* but was restless, eager to start a novel. He was back in New York by October 1892, living in a shabby boardinghouse with a crowd of medical students. He shared a room with Frederic Lawrence, a friend from Syracuse days and now in his last year of medical school. From their window they could look out over the roofs to the East River and Blackwell's Island, where prisoners marched in lockstep—a detail he shortly worked into *Maggie*.

Crane rarely went into the more respectable sections of the city, often talking of "the intense loneliness of being among the hordes of America's middle classes." He wandered the slums, or lounged about the room, smoking, writing, and reading. Sometimes Lawrence accompanied him on a tour of the mean streets. They would walk down the Bowery, then farther southeast where hordes of Jews, Italians, and Irish burrowed in the rooms of smelly tenements. Everything fascinated Crane—the swarm of humanity, the derelicts and toughs, wan-looking children and women wasted by age thirty, the swirl and din of horse-drawn wagons, street brawls, peddlers, the elevated, and clanging fire engines—the mingle of smells of poverty and vice and the commerce of the city. At night they were often in beer halls like the Bowery's Atlantic Gardens or Blank's near Fourteenth Street, or at one of the music halls like Koster & Bial's on Twenty-third Street.

Years later Lawrence remembered that Crane came in from one of his excursions in high excitement. "Did you ever see a stone fight?" he asked, and launched into a description of one he had just seen outside a tenement. "A little later that same day," Lawrence said, "the description had been set down on paper, and the first chapter of *Maggie* was written."

But there had been at least two previous drafts of the book. In March 1892 Crane had taken the manuscript to Richard Watson Gilder, editor of *Century Magazine.* It shocked Gilder. It seemed daring and filled with good touches, but he thought it "cruel and too profane." When he gave Crane his judgment the next day, the twenty-year-old cut him short—"You mean it's too honest." Gilder merely nodded and Crane left. He rewrote *Maggie*, but when it failed to interest other publishers he locked it in a box in Edmund's house.

In the room he shared with Lawrence, Crane began the version that was finally published. He filled page after page, writing for long stretches. Lawrence described his working routine:

> For a long time he would sit rapt in thought, devising his next sentence. Not until it had been completely formulated would he put pen to paper. Then he wrote slowly, carefully, in that legible round hand, with every punctuation mark accentuated, that always characterized his manuscripts. Rarely if ever did a word or mark require correction. A sentence completed, he would rise, relight his pipe, walk around the room or look out the window. He was usually silent, but sometimes he would break into some popular or bawdy song while he waited for inspiration to come. Sometimes he worked a whole day over a page and seldom wrote more than two or three.

Crane barely managed to keep himself alive. He borrowed freely from friends as well as his brothers, was poorly clothed, and often hungry. Helen remembered

that he would show up unexpectedly, "smelling of tobacco and looking like a drowned cat. He usually stayed
until he got tired of the family nagging him for fooling
away his time on the East Side with that driftwood of
humanity. . . . He never had a clean shirt . . . and most
of the time his toes were coming through his shoes 'most
lamentably' as he expressed it. His old gray coat would
have made a good stable mop, but was scarcely good for
anything else."

That kind of life was necessary, he felt, if he was to
write the truth. "I decided the nearer a writer gets to life,
the greater he becomes as an artist." Louis Senger, one
of his camping friends from Port Jervis, visited Crane in
New York. He was uneasy when he saw the reckless
disorder in the boardinghouse and thought the medical
students "a crowd of irresponsibles." But when Senger
read the *Maggie* manuscript, he was sharply aware of
Crane's genius for seeing "the ordinary and familiar with
first eyes," and he had a true sense of the book's importance.

Crane began showing the book to editors in February
1893. Willis Johnson of the *Tribune* was impressed by
the "throbbing vitality and dynamics of the story," but
warned him it would be hard to find a reputable publisher
since it would shock the "Podsnaps and Mrs. Grundys"
and bring on him "a storm of condemnation." After a few
unsuccessful tries, Crane, impatient to see it in print,
decided to publish it himself. He would use a pseudonym
so he wouldn't compromise his future or embarrass his
brothers and their prudish wives.

His mother had left each child equal shares of the Pennsylvania coal-mine stock. Crane sold his shares and ordered 1,100 copies of the book from a Sixth Avenue printer. He chose the name Johnson Smith (printed "Johnston" by mistake on the ugly mustard yellow cover).

"You see," Crane later said, "I was going to wait until the world was all on fire about Johnson Smith's 'Maggie' and then I was going to flop down like a trapeze performer from a wire, and coming forward with all the modest grace of a consumptive nun, say, *I am he, friends!* . . ."

The printing bill was $896, though he had typeset the pages himself to hurry publication, and he had to borrow from Will to pay it. He later learned that the printer, who specialized in religious and medical books, overcharged him by about $700. "You may take this," he wrote a friend, "as evidence of my imbecility. Will made me get the thing copyrighted. I had not even that much sense." The first edition of *Maggie: A Girl of the Streets* went on sale in March 1893 and cost fifty cents, but no bookstore or newsstand would touch it. Brentano's bookstore then relented, took twelve copies and returned ten. A maid at the boardinghouse used some copies from a pile in Crane's room to light a fire. A story circulated for years that Crane hired men to ride the elevated and trolleys reading *Maggie*, but it wasn't true.

He wrote an inscription across the paper cover of the copy he sent to Hamlin Garland:

"It is inevitable that you will be greatly shocked by

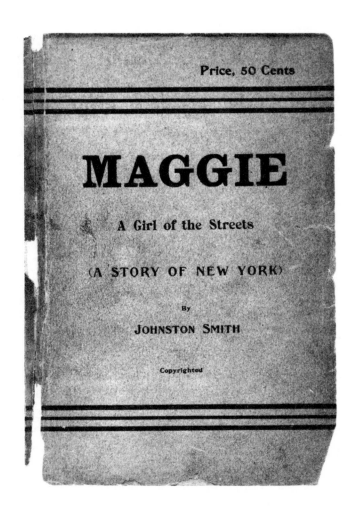

Price, 50 Cents

MAGGIE

A Girl of the Streets

(A STORY OF NEW YORK)

By

JOHNSTON SMITH

Copyrighted

Cover of the first edition of Maggie: A Girl of the Streets,
published by Crane in 1893 and using a pseudonym

George Arents Research Library,
Syracuse University

this book, but continue please with all possible courage to the end. For it tries to show that environment shapes lives regardless. If one proves that theory one makes room in Heaven for all sorts of souls (notably an occasional street girl) who are not expected to be there. It is probably that the reader of this small thing may consider the author to be a bad man, but obviously that is a matter of small consequence to the author."

There had been other novels and crusading moral tracts that dealt with the degradation of pure young slum girls. Crane's plot and theme were not much different. A description of the plot makes it sound more like sentimental melodrama than literary art.

The book tells the story of Maggie Johnson, a young girl who works in a factory. Her brother Jimmy is a Bowery truck driver. The mother, Mary, is an occasional prostitute who goes on drunken rampages. She beats her children, then smothers them with maudlin affection. The brooding father protests the beatings, but only because they disturb the peace. The sick baby, Tommy, dies of abuse and neglect. Jimmy bullies the world from a high seat on his van, bawling threats and curses at pedestrians and other drivers. He hangs out on street corners with Pete, a swaggering bartender. Maggie sees Pete as a fascinating man of the world who will take her away from her sordid existence. She yields to his advances, the mother throws her out, and she seeks Pete's protection. But he quickly tires of her, and when he turns her out, she becomes a prostitute. One evening, in despair, she turns from the bright avenue down a dark street to the river and drowns herself. When Jimmy brings the news to the mother, she bawls to the women of the tenement, "Oh, yes, I'll fergive her! I'll fergive her!"

What made *Maggie* a landmark in American fiction was Crane's style. "The steady phrase-by-phrase concentration, the steady brilliance, and the large design," said the poet John Berryman in his 1950 biography of Crane, "initiated modern American writing." Crane's method was radically new. He cast aside the familiar devices and conventions of fiction. He abandoned the usual narrative order and told the story in a series of loosely related episodes. "The picture he makes," said novelist Frank Norris, his contemporary, "is not a single composed painting, but rather many tiny flashlight photographs—instantaneous, caught, as it were, on the run."

Crane's powerful imagination was a shock to readers. His compressed scenes are written in short, vivid sentences and have odd turns of phrase, unexpected metaphors, and strange perspectives. Crane said he intended the book to be a work of realism about city squalor and human viciousness. "I had no other purpose in writing 'Maggie' than to show people as they seem to me. If that be evil, make the most of it." He had, of course, another and deeper intention. He makes only a few concessions to literal realism. His slum world is a flurry of images— the dreamlike tenement "looming with its hundred windows and dozen gruesome doorways" that spew "loads of babies into the street and gutter." A saloon squats on a corner, its "open mouth calling seductively." The true villain may be the environment, but the center of the book lies in the psyches of its characters. Maggie is a victim not just because of poverty, but because she could not see the world clearly. She has pretensions—she compares Pete to "a golden sun"—and wistful longings— "her dim thoughts were often searching for far away lands where the little hills sing together in the morning."

Meanwhile, as the book went on sale, he was destitute. For a tobacconist's bill of $1.30, he gave the man a gift copy, inscribed "This story will not edify or improve you and may not even interest you." He was down to cadging a nickel for a plate of eggs from Edmund in his New York office. If he made several dollars for an article, he spent it at once. A few unbearable days he spent as a haberdashery clerk gave him an idea for a story. It told of a young clerk constantly interrupted by customers as he tries to read his steamy French romance. Crane was paid fifteen dollars for the story—and spent it that night on a champagne supper.

Within a few weeks it was clear that *Maggie* would not make his literary fame or fortune. "My first great disappointment was in the reception of *Maggie: A Girl of the Streets*," he later wrote. "I remember how I looked forward to its publication, and pictured the sensation I thought it would make. It fell flat. Nobody seemed to notice it or care for it. . . . Poor 'Maggie'! She was one of my first loves." He hoped for a while that it might catch the attention of a regular publisher, but *Maggie*, it appeared, was dead.

Crane, however, had won the admiration of Hamlin Garland and William Dean Howells. "Well at least I've done something," he wrote to Lily Munroe. "I wrote a book. . . . Hamlin Garland was the first to overwhelm me with all manner of extraordinary language. The book has also made me a powerful friend in W. D. Howells. So I think I can say that if I 'watch out,' I'm almost a success. And 'such a boy, too' everyone writes."

When he confessed to Garland that he had written the book, the latter gave it a superb review in the literary magazine *Arena*, ending with "Crane has the genius to make an old world new." He sent a copy to Howells, who greatly admired and praised it. Here was the novel he had been asking for—the novel of social and moral intention that portrays the "familiar and low" and not "the great, the remote, the romantic." He invited Crane to lunch with other literary men, and introduced him as "a writer who has sprung into life fully armed." When talk got around to Samuel Clemens (Mark Twain), Howells said, "Crane can do things that Clemens can't." A power in the literary world, Howells tried to get bookstores to stock *Maggie* and sent copies to ministers interested in slum conditions. ("Maniacs for reform," Crane called them.) When they refused to acknowledge the book, it intensified his hatred of all "hypocritical religion."

Newspaper critics recognized Crane's talent and power, but almost all revealed the priggishness still common then. The *New York Press*: "It is a question if such brutalities are wholly acceptable in literature." The *New York Advertiser*: "He has success in drawing characters absolutely true to life, they are enough to give one the creeps." The *Philadelphia Press*: "Cold, awful, brutal realism. . . . But it is possible to tell a story of realism quite as suggestive and not so shocking as that told in Mr. Crane's book." John Barry, editor of the *Forum*, wrote to Crane: "It is pitilessly real and it produced its effect on me—the effect, I presume, that you wished to produce, a kind of horror. To be frank with you, I doubt if such literature is good. It closely approaches the morbid, and the morbid is always dangerous. . . ."

Crane's confidence, however, was unshaken. *Maggie* would later be hailed as a watershed in American literature—and what keeps it alive today with such savage force is the art that lies at its heart. Crane's real power was to make the reader see what he saw—and imagined.

Four

With *Maggie: A Girl of the Streets*, Stephen Crane struck
one of the first and fiercest blows against the genteel
tradition. In 1893, the country was prosperous, smug,
relaxed, hungry for novelty. Americans were ready for
any showy display and eager for any diversion appropri-
ate to their newfound wealth. But beneath the surface
of that confident middle-class world, of affluence, repression, and romance, there was a growing uncertainty, a
fear, a sense of tragedy to come. With his innovative style,
vivid irony, and psychological realism, Crane anticipated
and influenced writers who followed decades later. Ernest Hemingway, F. Scott Fitzgerald, Willa Cather, William Faulkner, Sherwood Anderson, Sinclair Lewis, John
Dos Passos, and John Steinbeck all owe something to
Crane. They also recognized this other America, flawed
by greed and injustice, by the great chasm between ide-
als and reality.

Crane and his artist friend Corwin Knapp Linson on the roof of Linson's studio, 1894

George Arents Research Library,
Syracuse University

*   *   *

In April 1893 Crane was living in a boardinghouse on Fifteenth Street in Manhattan. But he spent most of his time in the studios of C. K. Linson and other artists living in the old Art Students League building, a massive, gloomy structure on East Twenty-third Street. Its upper floors were occupied by artists, writers, and musicians, young men and women who welcomed the low rents and congenial atmosphere. A line from Ralph Waldo Emerson chalked on a beam in one of the studios particularly appealed to Crane—"Congratulate yourself if you have done something strange and extravagant and broken the monotony of a decorous age"—and he copied it into a pocket notebook. He wrote a comic story and Linson did the illustrations, but nothing came of it because a careless editor lost the artwork. He sold little that year but enjoyed life, and also continued to write poetry. He gave up his room and bummed a bed wherever he could in the league building, ate in the cheapest places, spent some time during the summer with his brothers, then went back to the same routine in the city.

Despite America's optimism and seeming prosperity, the country was plunged into an economic depression in the winter of 1893. It was the worst in the history of the country until the depression of the 1930s. For weeks Crane's only food was the "free lunch" in saloons. He and his friends often stayed in bed on bitterly cold days to keep warm because they couldn't afford firewood. While Linson painted on towels because he had no

Crane in Corwin Knapp Linson's art studio, where he began writing The Red Badge of Courage *in 1893*

George Arents Research Library,
Syracuse University

money for canvas, Crane huddled in a corner, a blanket around his shoulders, as he worked on a new book.

Crane had often looked through Linson's copies of *Century Magazine* that contained feature articles on "Battles and Leaders of the Civil War" for inspiration. He originally intended to write a potboiler about war, written quickly to earn some money—"something that would interest the boarding school element." He wrote a friend: "I have spent ten nights writing a story of the Civil War on my own responsibility, but I am not sure that my facts are real and the books won't tell me what I want to know so I must do it all over again, I guess."

The matter-of-fact accounts by veterans of the war annoyed him. "I wonder that some of these fellows didn't tell how they *felt* in those scrapes!" he said to Linson. "They spout eternally of what they *did*, but they are as emotionless as rocks!" He knew the facts of warfare from his long obsession with the military, but he wanted to know the relationship between feeling and fact as revealed by a soldier in crisis. He had read Tolstoy's *Sebastapol* and came to realize that that antiheroic novel of the Crimean War would give him the model for the new book—not the pedestrian memoirs of ex-soldiers.

While he struggled with *The Red Badge of Courage*, Crane looked for work. One day he was in the office of Edward Marshall, Sunday editor of the *New York Press*. Crane had been wearing rubber boots without shoes but bought a pair of cheap shoes and tramped without an overcoat to the interview in a rainstorm. "I'll take all the special articles you can do," Marshall said, "but you are made for better things. Don't waste your time." Too proud to tell the editor he didn't have a nickel for carfare, Crane walked back to Twenty-third Street. He was shivering and weak and spent the next week in bed. He worked on some New York sketches that Marshall took for five dollars a column and that kept him going for a while. Hamlin Garland tried to get him work and sent him to S. S. McClure, publisher and editor of *McClure's* magazine with a personal note, "If you have anything for Mr. Crane, talk things over with him, and for mercy's sake don't keep him *standing* for an hour as you did before." A few days later Crane wrote to Lily Munroe:

> They used to call me "that terrible young rascal," but now they are beginning to hem and haw and smile—those very old coots who used to condescend to me. Once McClure kept me waiting for an hour and then made a cool apology I wouldn't have used on a dog. When he caught sight of me in the outer office the other day he came out of his private office. "Ah, Crane, my dear boy, come in and have a cigar and chat." He quickly got rid of an author who was haggling over a story. I wonder if he considered that I had lost my memory. "No—thanks—I'm in a hurry." He seemed really grieved.

McClure, however, knew Crane was a superior talent and offered to send him on several assignments. First would be a few weeks in Europe where he could roam and observe the scene and write what he wanted. Garland and Howells objected to the European trip, saying Crane was wasting his time in journalism. Crane decided not to leave New York until he had seen at least one more book go into print—and never went to Europe for McClure.

He continued his explorations of the Bowery and slums, sometimes disappearing for days, then returning exhausted and ill, looking like the derelicts he studied. Linson saw him walk into the studio one morning, soaked, toes coming out of his shoes. "As if reading my thoughts, Crane looked at me and grinned. A hollow cough racked his body, but he said, 'How can I know how these poor devils feel if I was warm myself? Anyway, you mutt, I don't have any more clothes.' " Another friend thought he would be taken care of and able to write if he married. He suggested it to Crane, who scoffed, "Marriage is a base trick on women, who are hunted animals anyway."

During this time, he produced two of his finest stories: "An Experiment in Misery" and "The Men in the Storm." In the former, he "tried to make plain that the root of Bowery life is a sort of cowardice. Perhaps I mean a lack of ambition or to willingly be knocked flat and accept the licking." But he always drew the difference between men of "patience, industry, and temperance" who are merely down on their luck, and the shiftless drunks and derelicts of the Bowery.

When working on the Civil War book, he occasionally wrote articles for the *New York Press*, but his financial condition was little improved when he took a room on West Thirty-third Street. He wanted to show Garland his poetry and wrote to him: "I have not been to see you because of various strange conditions—notably, my toes are coming through one shoe and I have not been going out in society as much as I might." Linson called on him one day to see why he hadn't been to the studio, and found he was a virtual prisoner because he had no shoes. Linson bought him a pair.

Garland thought the poetry was superb. It was a series of poems later published as *The Black Riders*. They were all on religious themes: the inscrutability of God, man's futile quest for God, God's wrath, the terrors of a godless universe, man's sin and guilt. The old issues about God and man preached from the Methodist pulpits of Crane's childhood obviously lingered on. When Garland complimented him, Crane pointed to his temple and said, "I've got five or six more in a little row up here. That's the way they come—in little rows, all made up, ready to be put down on paper." Garland was skeptical and asked Crane to do one for him. Crane sat down at the desk, and "it flowed from his pen like oil, one of his most powerful poems," Garland wrote.

In April 1894 Crane saw Garland again and showed him a manuscript. It was the first part of *Private Fleming, His Various Battles*, later retitled *The Red Badge of Courage*. Garland was immediately caught, stunned by the opening:

> The cold passed reluctantly from the earth, and the retiring fogs revealed an army stretched out on the hills, resting. As the landscape changed from brown to green, the army awakened, and began to tremble with eagerness at the noise of rumors. It cast its eyes upon the roads, which were growing from long troughs of liquid mud to proper thoroughfares. A river, amber-tinted in the shadow of its banks, purled at the army's feet; and at night, when the stream had become of a sorrowful blackness, one could see across it the red, eyelike gleam of hostile camp-fires set in the low brows of distant hills.

The first page of the manuscript of The Red Badge of Courage
Clifton Waller Barrett Collection,
Alderman Library, University of Virginia

But Crane had brought only half the manuscript. "Where is the rest? We must get it published at once." Crane, embarrassed, said it was "in hock to the typist for $15." Garland gave him the money and read the complete manuscript. He recommended the work to S. S. Mc-Clure, who was sure he could use it either for distribution to his newspaper syndicate or as a serial in *McClure's* magazine.

Garland wrote that the "opening took me captive. It described a vast army in camp on one side of a river, confronting with its thousands of eyes a similar monster on the opposite bank. The finality which lay in every word, the epic breadth of vision, the splendor of the pictures presented—all indicates a most powerful and original imagination as well as a mature mastery of literary form. Crane's imagery transforms the commonplace conventions of the Civil War story into literature. I experienced the thrill of the editor who has fallen unexpectedly upon the work of a genius. It was as if the youth in some mysterious way had secured the cooperation of a spirit, the spirit of an officer in the Civil War. How else could one account for the boy's knowledge of war? I spoke of this, and in his succinct, self-derisive way he candidly confessed that all his knowledge of battle had been gained on the football field."

The book's subtitle is *An Episode of the American Civil War*. The setting and action seem to be based on the Battle of Chancellorsville fought in May 1863, but it is really about the landscape of fear in one soldier's mind during his baptism of combat. *The Red Badge of Courage* was nothing less than Crane's challenge to deeply felt American beliefs. The folklore built on romantic memories of the Civil War was Shakespeare and the *Iliad* for the American village. It gave its inhabitants a sense of identity and share achievement, and strengthened their confidence in the American past and future. But Crane—long before the disillusioned poets of World War I—spoke of the chauvinism and patriotic humbug that glorified the "honor" and "self-sacrifice" of war.

The book would become an American classic, a work in which Stephen Crane tapped for the first time the full powers of his imagination.

The Red Badge of Courage is the story of young Henry Fleming from a small town in Ohio. Inflamed by patriotic speeches and tales from the battlefield, he enlists to save the Union. He is vain, pretentious, the victim of heroic illusions, and longs to prove himself. He becomes impatient with the routine, the troop movements that seem without purpose, and the incompetence of generals. He aches to get at the hated enemy. Just as battle is about to begin, Henry Fleming feels himself "an unknown quantity . . . continually trying to measure himself by his comrades, looking for kindred emotions," yet at the same time with the sense of being "separated from the others."

In his first action, he stands up under fire and his confidence and bragging grow. But in the next engagement, he bolts to the rear in terror and is clubbed in the head by a soldier trying to stem the tide of deserters from the battlefield. The wound is his "red badge." He returns to his unit with his head bandaged and fights fiercely.

His fellow soldiers are either dead or have come to terms with the reality of combat and their own character. Henry Fleming never does. He had expected his war to be "Greek-like struggles," fanfare and glory. He found instead that it was death, mutilation, filth, chaos, and boredom. He seems to have accepted this—but he has only replaced his romantic notions with an equally romantic pose of the battle-hardened soldier. He thinks his cowardice has been redeemed, but he is still vulnerable to his illusions. In Crane's view, Henry Fleming has fled once like "a rabbit." The next time, Crane hints, he might flee like a lion.

Professor James Nagel in his *Stephen Crane and Literary Impressionism* calls it "the first monumental impressionistic novel in American literature . . . the finest piece of extended fiction that Crane ever wrote. . . . His sensory emphasis makes reading the novel seem more a visual than a verbal experience." The book makes use of color and other pictorial effects. Like Impressionist paintings, it conveys a feeling of reality in constant change, as the mood or point of view of the observer changes from moment to moment. What is so striking and new in *Red Badge* is that everything seen is observed through the anxiety-distorted mind of Henry Fleming.

His psychological struggle is dramatized in imagery that seems to make the terror of war and the terror of nature the same. Mountains, fields and streams, the night and sun, appear to him as living creatures, monstrous and fearsome. He sees the "red eye-like gleam of hostile campfires" . . . black columns of enemy troops disappearing over a hill "like two serpents crawling from the cavern of light." When his regiment crosses a stream marching to the front, he thinks the water below the bridge looks at him with "white bubble-eyes." He imagines "fierce-eyed hosts" lurking in the shadowed woods. When he runs to the rear, he flees not so much the enemy as "the onslaught of redoubtable dragons." He sees "red and green monsters" that seem to spring out of the earth.

In a peaceful forest, he reaches a secluded place where "high, arching boughs made a chapel." It is, he supposes, a retreat provided by a tender Mother Nature for his spiritual comfort. He pushes aside "green doors" and is suddenly horrified—sitting on the "gentle brown carpet" in the "religious half-light" is a rotting corpse. As he bolts, Nature suddenly seems to turn on him in a fury, snagging branches try to draw him back to the corpse. Once after a furious fight, he glances upward and feels "a flash of astonishment at the blue, pure sky and the sun-gleamings on the trees and fields." He finds it "surprising that nature has gone tranquilly on with her golden processes in the midst of so much devilment." Henry Fleming is never sure whether Nature is hostile or sympathetic, or merely indifferent. And not knowing, he has no way of fixing his place in the scheme of things.

In the novel, Stephen Crane wrote one of the most famous metaphors in American literature—"The red sun was pasted in the sky like a wafer." It was a striking image, but for Crane, it also meant the blood of war ("the red animal, war . . .). It occurs when Henry Fleming sees Jim Conklin, the "tall soldier," die, his body looking "as if it had been chewed up by wolves."

> The youth turned, with sudden, livid rage, toward the battlefield. He shook his fist. He seemed about to deliver a curse.
> "Hell——"
> The red sun was pasted in the sky like a wafer.

Crane was certain that McClure would publish the novel and turned to other work. He wrote a Memorial Day article for the *New York Press* on a parade of Civil War veterans. He celebrated "the fidelity to truth and duty" of the "brave, simple, quiet men who crowded upon the opposing bayonets of their country's enemies." Anxious to get away for a camping trip, Crane wrote the tribute weeks before the actual parade. It was a bad piece, limping from platitudes to sentimentality. The *Press* rejected it as "too intricate" for their readers. That late spring of 1894, he also started his third novel, *George's Mother*. He wrote Garland that he was eating "with charming regularity at least two times a day. I am content and am writing another novel which is a bird."

In June, McClure, with no word about publication of *Red Badge*, assigned him and Linson to do an illustrated article for his magazine on Pennsylvania coal mines. When it was printed, Crane was furious. McClure had tampered with it, cut out all his criticism of big business. "They didn't want the truth after all. Why the hell did

A photograph of Crane by Corwin Knapp Linson as a study for his oil portrait, 1894

Clifton Waller Barrett Collection,
Alderman Library, University of Virginia

The 1894 oil portrait of Crane by Corwin Knapp Linson
Clifton Waller Barrett Collection,
Alderman Library, University of Virginia

they send me up there then? So they want the public to think the coal mines gilded ballrooms with the miners eating ice cream in stiff shirt-fronts?" Years later Linson remembered Crane's work on the coal mines as "a painting . . . a great canvas of a dramatic solemnity."

That summer in Port Jervis with brother William's family was "sunny blue" for Crane except for one unpleasant incident. A malicious Port Jervis woman accused him of corrupting a thirteen-year-old girl he had taken for a buggy ride. There was nothing to the charge, and he took revenge by ridiculing the woman in two novels and a short story.

Returning to the city in October, he took a small room near the Art Students League and looked for work as a reporter. It was six months since he had given McClure the *Red Badge* manuscript. Nothing had happened and he took it back. "As a matter of fact," he wrote Garland, "I have just crawled out of the fifty-third ditch into which I have been cast and now I feel I can write you a letter that won't make you ill. McClure was a beast about the war novel. He kept it until I was nearly mad. Oh, yes, he was going to use it, but——."

Crane took the manuscript to the Irving Bacheller newspaper syndicate. He said he "needed money" and had "enough of just praise." Bacheller, who remembered Crane as "a frail boy of unusual modesty," read it that night and bought it for ninety dollars. He planned to syndicate the book in a severely cut version—the original 55,000 words cut to 18,000. Crane needed the money and it was better than nothing.

The Red Badge of Courage appeared first in the *Philadelphia Press* from December 3 through 8, then in a single issue of the *New York Press* of December 9. After that, it appeared in hundreds of small-city dailies and weeklies across the country. Though the novel was mutilated, it became instantly popular. One reason for its success was the novelty of a war story told from a private's point of view. Wars in earlier fiction were fought mainly by officers, gallants, and villains, noteworthy men who moved against a background of massed troops.

The literary editor of the *Philadelphia Press* was asked, "Who is this man Crane, anyhow?" He replied, "Well, if he keeps this up, we'll all know him in a few years." E. J. Edwards of the *New York Press* wrote that Crane was destined to become "the most powerful of America's teller of tales." Curtis Brown of the same paper met Crane near his office. "It was snowing and windy and he was without an overcoat, but his face—thin and white—lit up when he saw me. He threw his arms around me and said, 'Oh, do you think it was good?' Fortunately I could guess what he meant and said, 'It's great.' He said, 'God bless you' and hurried off in the snow."

But there was almost no reaction from the literary world. Crane wanted a reputable publisher to present the book as he wrote it and sent the manuscript to Ripley Hitchcock, an editor at Appleton & Company. Before he got any word from Appleton, he left on a trip to the West for the Bacheller syndicate as a roving correspondent. On January 30, 1895, he wrote Hitchcock from St. Louis,

Missouri, that "any news of the war story will be welcome." In mid-February, while in Lincoln, Nebraska, he got word that Appleton would publish the book. It was a turn in fortune that probably saved the novel from destruction. Crane later told a friend that he had decided to burn the manuscript if the publisher rejected it.

In almost three years of poverty and struggle, he had written four impressive, highly orignal books—*Maggie: A Girl of the Streets*, *The Black Riders*, *The Red Badge of Courage*, and the novel he had just finished, *George's Mother*. If he had known that one day they would be important landmarks in the history of American writing, he might have felt overjoyed at Hitchcock's news. But his answer was subdued: "I've just received your letter. I would be glad to have Appleton & Co. publish the story. I am going from here to New Orleans. The Mss. could be corrected by me there in short order."

In Lincoln, he met Willa Cather, who would later become one of America's greatest writers. She was a college student and journalist then, and an aspiring novelist. She worked for the *Nebraska State Journal* and had proofread the paper's syndicated version of *Red Badge*. Crane came to the office one day hoping to find a check from Bacheller. He was the first author she had met and she was surprised he was so unimpressive.

He was gaunt and unshaven. His gray clothes were much the worse for wear and fitted him badly. He wore a flannel shirt and a slovenly apology for a tie, and his shoes were dusty and worn at the toes and badly run over at the heels. He appeared as nervous as a race horse fretting to be on the track. . . . He always seemed like a man preparing for a sudden departure. I remember once when he was writing a letter, he asked me how to spell a word, saying "I haven't time to learn to spell," then glanced down at his attire and smiled, "I haven't time to dress either. It takes an awful slice out of a fellow's life."

They talked literature, but she sensed that he didn't take her seriously. "His talk was frivolous, absent-minded, and I thought he seemed bitter and depressed." On Crane's last night in Lincoln, she returned to the newspaper office and found him wandering in the hall. He was looking for Bacheller's check, but it still hadn't come.

> I have never known so bitter a heart in any man as he revealed to me that night. He confessed that he was bitterly despondent, and I was convinced that he had a vague pre-monition of the shortness of his life. . . . I said that in ten years he would probably laugh at his present bitterness, but Crane exclaimed, 'I can't wait ten years. I haven't time.'

Willa Cather never forgot his reply to her academic questions about how stories were constructed: "Where do you get all that rot? Yarns aren't done by mathematics. You can't do it by rule any more than you can dance by rule. You have to have the itch of the thing in your fingers, and if you haven't—well, you're damned lucky, and you'll live long and prosper, that's all!"

ℱive

Waiting for money in Lincoln, Crane lived hand to mouth for days. His time in the West, thus far, had been dismal. But he was to draw on his experiences there for two of his greatest short stories—"The Blue Hotel" and "The Bride Comes to Yellow Sky"—which he wrote three years later in England. Three incidents in Nebraska inspired the masterly "Blue Hotel."

The first was when he tried to break up a fistfight at the bar of the Hotel Lincoln. Then while covering the aftermath of a great drought in the western part of the state, he headed for a small town and was caught in a blizzard. The town, a straggle of dim and silent houses huddling in the savage wind, was deserted. In the countryside, he saw horses standing "abjectly and stolidly, their backs humped and turned toward the eye of the wind, heads near the ground, manes blowing over their eyes, the soft noses crusted with ice." When Crane asked a farmer how he got along, the man said, "Don't git along, stranger. Who the hell told you I did git along?" Then, while changing trains at a desolate junction town, he saw a hotel painted an unforgettable light blue. The hotel became the setting, and the blizzard, fight, and melancholy landscape figured large in the story.

He made the *Red Badge* corrections in New Orleans, Louisiana, then traveled through Arkansas, Texas, Arizona, and Nevada. Only a few years before, Frederick Turner, a Yale history professor, had pronounced the closing of the western frontier, the end of an era. Crane's dispatches confirmed it. He dwelled on how modern the West was, the advance of eastern civilization on the "Old Wild West," how raw plains towns were becoming cities. It was the theme at the heart of "The Bride Comes to Yellow Sky." He found that the Old West existed now largely in the romantic visions of travelers.

In San Antonio, Texas, he visited the Alamo. The chapel was defended by some 150 Texas revolutionaries when Santa Anna, the Mexican general, attacked on February 24, 1836. The siege lasted until March 6, when all the Texans lay dead. Crane called the Alamo "the greatest memorial to courage that civilization has allowed to stand." But he was more interested in the story of one Texan in the Alamo. After being told their fate was sealed and all must die, that man calmly said no, bid a last good-bye, and climbed the wall. For Crane, it was proof of the ambivalence of the heroic.

In Alamo Plaza, Crane saw a crying sixteen-year-old. The youth had run away to the West to be a cowboy and was penniless and stranded. Crane bought him a ticket home and later wrote him a bantering note in Bowery lingo:

"Dear Deadeye Dick: Thanks for sending my money back so fast. The hotel trun me out, as my Bowery friends say, and I was living in the Mex diggings with sheep men till my boss in New York wired me money. Now, take some advice from a tough jay from back east. You say your family is jake and nobody bothers you. Well, it struck me that you are too young a kid to be free and easy around where a lot of bad boys and girls will take your last pennies. So better stay home and grow a moustache before you hustle out into the red universe any more."

While in Arizona, he crossed the border into Mexico and was fascinated by the country. "One Dash—Horses" was a short story he wrote about an adventure there. He and his guide were asleep in a peasant village when bandits rode in. The two men slipped away to their horses and galloped off. The bandits gave chase and were gaining on them when they were rescued by a company of *federales*, the mounted police. He was back in New York in May 1895, his face "tanned the color of a brick sidewalk."

That summer he did some work for Bacheller but mostly marked time until *Red Badge* was published. A job as drama critic for the *Philadelphia Press* fell through, and he retreated to his brothers' homes in Hartwood and Port Jervis. After the exhausting western journey, and years of grinding city life, the quiet, rural villages were

Title page of The Red Badge of Courage, *1895*
Clifton Waller Barrett Collection,
Alderman Library, University of Virginia

a welcome change. He played games with his nieces, cops and robbers his favorite, and wore white flannels for croquet and tennis with young vacationers at the resort hotels. An excellent horseman, he rode the hill trails for hours. In the mornings, he often sat in a wicker chair on Will's front porch and wrote.

The Red Badge of Courage was published in October 1895. William Dean Howells gave the book an unenthusiastic review in *Harper's*. Other war writers, he said, had given a more realistic sense of battle, and though the book was "worthwhile on the psychological side," its greater significance was in its promise of better things to come "from a new talent working upon a high level, not quite clearly as yet, but strenuously." Crane never mentioned his disappointment. He knew that Howells thought the war novel a mistake, a diversion from serious literary work.

But within a month, reviews from all over the country hailed the book for its dramatic intensity and vivid imagery. It was the first nonromantic novel of the Civil War to become popular. The *Atlantic Monthly* pronounced it "great enough to start a new fashion in literature." The *New York Press* review was one of the most perceptive:

> His description of battle is so vivid as to be almost suffocating. The reader is right down in the midst where patriotism is dissolved into its elements and where only a dozen men can be seen, firing blindly and grotesquely into the smoke. This is war from a new point of view, and it seems more than when seen with an eye only for large

movements. . . . One should be slow to call an author a genius, but *The Red Badge of Courage* has greater power and originality than can be girdled by the mere name of talent.

Crane soon became internationally famous. An English publisher brought the novel out at the end of November, and it was soon one of that country's most popular books. The London literary publication *Critic* called it a little masterpiece, but found fault with Crane's grammar. Harold Frederic, novelist and London correspondent for the *New York Times*, wrote, "The book will be talked about more than anything else in current literature. It will be kept alive as one of those deathless books which must be read by everybody who desires to be a connoisseur of modern fiction. . . . It has no equals. It is a book outside of all classifications."

Joseph Conrad, one of the world's great writers, later said that the sensation Crane's book produced was one of the enduring memories of his literary life. H. G. Wells, already a popular writer, told how deeply the English literary world admired "its freshness of method, its vigor of imagination, its force of color and its essential freedom from many traditions."

Ford Madox Ford, who would become a famous novelist and editor, said, "In *The Red Badge* we are provided with a map that shows us our own hearts." In World War I, Ford and other soldiers read *The Red Badge* in the trenches during lulls in the fighting—in English or in French or German translations.

Crane at twenty-three, photographed during a trip to Washington, D.C., 1895

Clifton Waller Barrett Collection,
Alderman Library, University of Virginia

85

It was reviewed enthusiastically for months in English papers and literary magazines, which stimulated new interest in the book in America. Between January and June of 1896, it was on the best-seller list in every major city in the United States.

Some Civil War veterans who read the book were certain that they had known the author in the army. "I was with Crane at Antietam," Colonel John L. Burleigh told friends. Others were sure they had served with him at Chancellorsville or Malvern Hill. General Sir Evelyn Woods in the *Illustrated London News* said Crane's work was the finest thing that had ever been done, and that "the intentions of the boy who has never seen war are worth far more than any writer who may have been in the thick of the fiercest battle." Most American veterans said the book was absolutely faithful to the facts—but it was expected that some military men would object. General A. C. McClurg saw Crane's book as a vicious slander on American soldiers. He wrote a letter to *Dial* in response to the magazine's enthusiastic review:

> The hero of the book, if such he can be called, was an ignorant and stupid country lad without a spark of patriotic feeling or soldierly ambition. He is throughout an idiot or a maniac and betrays no trace of the reasoning being. No thrill of patriotic devotion to cause or country moves his breast, and not even an emotion of manly courage. Even a wound he gets comes from a comrade who strikes him on the head with a musket to get rid of him; and this is the only "Red Badge of Courage" (!) which we discover in

the book. It is the work of a young man, and so of course it must be a mere work of diseased imagination. . . . Soldier Fleming is a coward, a Northerner who fled the field . . . and that is why the British have praised the book.

The book went into a fourth edition, and Crane for the first time was making money from his writing. But his happiness over his success was short-lived. Editors deluged him with requests for war stories. McClure wanted a series about famous Civil War battlefields. After a hurried visit to the Fredericksburg battlefield, Crane rejected the offer. He was little interested in becoming a military historian or writing more war fiction. "Hang all war stories . . . that damned *Red Badge*," he wrote to a woman friend. "I once thought it a pretty good thing, but now I no longer care for it."

Many American and English literary figures argued over who discovered Crane first. He said he was flattered, glad he was discovered, but thought it probable "only one Columbus could have discovered me." He was besieged by fans whenever he was in New York to see editors, and often rushed away in a kind of panic without keeping the appointments. McClure thought he might do a novel about politics and sent him to Washington, D.C., to study the scene. But Crane quickly gave up the idea after talking to many senators and representatives. "These people pose so hard, that it would take a double-barreled shotgun to disclose their inward feelings, and I despair of knowing them." Appleton wanted to republish *Maggie*, and so Crane began revising it. He gave *George's*

Mother to a different publisher, violating, as he admitted, "certain business courtesies."

Grim and unsparing, *George's Mother* is modern in its story of a destructive relationship. Set in the slums, as was *Maggie*, it is, however, a far more sophisticated book. It tells of a possessive, fanatically religious mother's ruination of her son. She believes him to be brilliant, destined for greatness. But the son neither lives up to her expectations nor fulfills his own dreams. Mother and son live in their own worlds with no communication. Alcohol and the flattery of his saloon friends feed the son's growing resentment of his mother's nagging and moralizing. He becomes callous and abusive to her, then loses his job. He tries to borrow money from his friends, but they desert him and he joins a gang of toughs. When George gets word that this mother is dying, he is fighting for a share in a stolen bucket of beer.

While writing it, Crane told a friend, "This book will leave *Maggie* at the post. It is my best thing." Some critics thought it up to his best work, but it was the English critic Edward Garnett who hailed *George's Mother* as "a masterpiece . . . The rare thing about Mr. Crane's art is that he keeps closer to the surface than any living writer, and like the great portrait-painters, to a great extent makes the surface betray the depths." Today the book is understood to be an extraordinary, pioneering work.

Crane wrote over twenty articles for the McClure and Bacheller syndicates throughout the summer of 1896. In September, he moved to a boardinghouse rented mostly by prostitutes. With growing fame, he had to fight off accusations that he was an opium addict and drunk who "bedded degraded women." Much of the libel was the work of Edgar Saltus, a writer jealous of Crane's success. "A man sometimes yearns to write vulgar inanity and sell it by the carload to fools," he wrote in a letter to a newspaper. "I hear that Stephen Crane has made twenty thousand dollars out of his trash." Crane had little idea of how much money he was making, happy only that he could draw one hundred dollars from Appleton at any time.

The *New York Journal* hired him to do a series of articles on the Tenderloin. Extending a block east and west of Sixth Avenue from Fourteenth Street to Forty-second Street, the Tenderloin was the uptown, higher-priced version of the Bowery, and no less dangerous. It had anything a man could pay for—prostitutes, sex shows, drugs, gambling, saloons, dance halls, and theaters. The name came from Police Captain Alexander "Clubber" Williams. After years in a quiet area, he was shifted to command of the district's police. Hinting at the graft paid police, he gloated, "I been eatin' the chuck for a long time, and now I'm gonna get me some of the tenderloin." Crane sat in police court and at night roamed the gaslit streets to look in on "unsavory resorts," like the Turkish Parlors and Broadway Gardens. One night he became involved in a notorious affair that brought him the bitter and undying hatred of the New York police.

About 2:00 A.M. on September 16 Crane was on a Broadway corner with two chorus girls and a prostitute named Dora Clark. Dora and one of the chorus girls waited while Crane escorted the other across the street to a trolley car. A policeman in civilian clothes approached the two women and arrested them for soliciting men who had just walked by. Crane saw the struggling women being taken away, and protested. The chorus girl suddenly became hysterical and screamed, pointing at Crane, "But he's my husband!" Crane, hoping to help the woman, said he was. The policeman released her, but took Dora Clark to the West Thirtieth Street station house. Crane and the chorus girl followed and protested to the desk sergeant. He tried to give Crane good advice about defending a known prostitute.

"If you monkey with this case, you are pretty sure to come out with mud all over you."

"I suppose so," Crane said. "I haven't any doubt of it. But I don't see how I can, in honesty, stay away from court in the morning."

It was a story that made headline news for weeks. Crane publicly accused the patrolman, Charles Becker, of false arrest. The *Journal* hailed Crane as a hero who "showed the red badge of courage" in risking "the censure of thousands who admire his books by manfully championing a woman of whom he knew nothing." Crane's own full-page account of the incident appeared in the *Journal* three days later. Editorials in many papers condemned the police.

Matters grew worse in October when Dora Clark brought charges against Becker for false arrest and assault. She claimed that a few days after her release, he had attacked her one night until "bystanders interfered and Becker went." Crane testified at Becker's trial. In a painful cross-examination by the policeman's lawyer, he had to deny that he ran an "opium joint" in his room and "habitually consorted with prostitutes." Angry and humiliated, Crane sent a telegram of protest to Police Commissioner Theodore Roosevelt. Editorials strongly condemned the judge for permitting the lawyer to abuse Crane about matters that had nothing to do with the case. Roosevelt, who admired Crane's work, ignored the telegram. A result of the case, said a friend, "was that an aroused and a resentful police department tried in every way to discredit Crane and made New York finally too hot for him by their constant harassment."

Becker became an important footnote in the history of New York crime. In 1913 he shot gambler Herman Rosenthal outside a Times Square hotel. Rosenthal had threatened to expose Becker's own partnership in a gambling operation and his strong connection with the underworld. He was electrocuted two years later, the first New York City policeman to be sentenced to death.

Crane wanted to get out of New York. His reputation had suffered, and there seemed little to hold him in the city. Bacheller offered him a job as a war correspondent, and Crane jumped at it. Cuba was revolting against its Spanish colonial masters, and Bacheller wanted Crane to join the rebel guerrillas. It was a hard and dangerous assignment, but at the moment nothing suited Crane's purposes better. In mid-November, carrying seven hundred dollars in gold in a money belt, he departed for

Jacksonville, Florida, elated at the prospect of seeing real war at last.

Crane reached Jacksonville on November 14, 1896, and registered under a false name at the hotel, afraid his recent notoriety had followed him. He tried to arrange passage to Cuba on a "filibuster" (guerrilla) ship. He would be landed on some remote Cuban beach where the contraband arms were unloaded, then make his way past Spanish patrols to the Cuban rebels in the country's interior. It was risky—Spanish gunboats patrolled the Cuban waters, and the journey to the rebels was even more dangerous. The Spanish looked on American journalists as spies and had captured several and imprisoned them for months.

One night, while waiting to sail, Crane went to a "fashionable" night club, the Hotel de Dream. It was actually a discreet, plush brothel on the outskirts of the city run by a woman named Cora Stewart Taylor. The daughter of a Massachusetts painter and cultured mother, she had been married twice, the second time to a British army officer. She had spent some time in India where her husband commanded the British forces, but she found the life disagreeable. Separated but still married, she mysteriously appeared in Jacksonville, made over an old hotel, and went into business. E. W. Cready, the *New York Herald* correspondent, remembered her as "handsome, of some real refinement, aloof to most—to all indeed until Steve arrived." Six years older than the twenty-five-year-old Crane, she was literary and intelligent and found the young writer-adventurer irresistible.

Cora Crane in 1892, four years before she met Stephen Crane in Jacksonville, Florida

George Arents Research Library,
Syracuse University

They discussed literature, spent more and more time together, and quickly became lovers. He became the ruling passion of her life.

Passage for Crane was arranged on the *Commodore* being readied for a run to Cuba with a cargo of arms, ammunition, and rebels. On December 31, 1896, he boarded the large seagoing tug and she sailed at dusk. Two miles down the St. John River, she ran aground on a sandbar in a heavy fog. The *Commodore* had to wait until morning for the U.S. revenue cutter *Boutwell* to pull her out of the mud. Ironically, the cutter was on station to prevent any ship from slipping past and violating American neutrality in the Cuban uprising. The tug ran aground again but dragged herself free by her own power and at last gained the open sea.

The first night at sea, Crane was in the pilothouse with Captain Edward Murphy, when the chief engineer reported trouble below. The *Commodore*'s hull had been damaged in the groundings and water was rising fast in the engine room. The pumps couldn't keep up with the flooding, and Crane went below to help bail with a large bucket. "The engine room was a scene from the kitchen of Hell . . . lights burned faintly in a way to cause mystic and gruesome shadows." The scorching heat drove Crane topside. Captain Murphy ordered wood, oil, and alcohol fed to the boiler to get up enough steam to reach the nearest land, eighteen miles due west.

There was panic aboard. A stoker came up from the hold with dynamite and said they should set it off. The explosive was gingerly taken from him, then Murphy smashed him in the face. A hysterical sailor climbed the rigging and tried to stand on his head on a spar. A Cuban tried to jump overboard but was overpowered. Another kneeled at the captain's feet and begged to be thrown into the sea. A man tried to launch one of the small boats before time and Crane knocked him down. Captain Murphy later said:

> That man Crane is the spunkiest fellow out. When we got off the sandbar into the open sea we hit very rough water. Many men got seasick but Crane was like an old sailor. . . . When the leak was discovered, he was the first man to volunteer to help. He stood fast on the deck with me, smoking a cigarette, and helped me greatly when the boats were trying to get off. When in the dinghy he suggested putting up his overcoat for a sail, and he took his turn at the oars or holding up the mast. . . . He's a thoroughbred.

Murphy sent the Cubans off in two of the three big lifeboats, and most of the crew in the third. Murphy, Crane, the cook, and an oiler named Higgins got off in the ten-foot dinghy. At dawn, they discovered that seven crewmen were still aboard the floundering tug. Their lifeboat had been damaged in the launching but they had managed to reboard the ship. They had improvised small rafts and put them in the water, but with sharks around, they were hesitant to jump. Crane and the others shouted encouragement and tried to beat off the sharks. Four men dived into the water, but only three reached the rafts. The first mate never surfaced after he hit the water. Suddenly the *Commodore* swung wildly into the wind, rolled, and plunged bow down into the sea, dragging the rafts and three men under. The three still aboard were leaning against the deckhouse, strangely casual, as the tug went under.

Twelve miles west across the sea, the Mosquito Inlet lighthouse "stuck above the horizon like the point of a pin." The dinghy reached the coast south of Daytona, Florida, late that afternoon. Murphy thought the surf too high for a landing, and Crane and Billy Higgins at the oars took the craft out to sea again. They kept about the same distance from shore throughout the night, and by midmorning the wind and current had carried them north toward Daytona. Murphy decided to try a run through the boiling surf. The dinghy capsized, striking Higgins in the head. Crane shucked his heavy money belt and tried to help him, but Higgins drowned. A man on the beach plunged into the surf and helped the exhausted men to shore. When reporters rushed to the scene, Charles Montgomery, the cook, added his estimate of Crane:

> That newspaper fellow was a nervy man. He didn't seem to know what fear was. . . . He signed on as an able seaman at twenty dollars a month, insisted on doing a seaman's work, and did it well. He never quailed when he saw the raging waves and knew the vessel was sinking, and that it was only a matter of time when we would be at the mercy of the sea in a small dinghy. He stood on the bridge with glasses in hand, sweeping the horizon for some

glimpse of land. . . . I thought sure he'd be swept off because the vessel was rolling hard, her spars almost touching the water.

Crane was in the news again, and one headline read: YOUNG NEW YORK WRITER ASTONISHED THE SEA DOGS BY HIS COURAGE IN THE FACE OF DEATH. Crane's own account, syndicated by Bacheller, appeared in the *New York Press* on January 7, 1897. Cora, frantic since first hearing news of the wreck, came to take Crane back to Jacksonville. In the hotel lobby, he signed one of his books for a nine-year-old girl, "Stephen Crane, able seaman S. S. *Commodore.*"

While he recuperated, Crane wrote his short-story masterpiece, "The Open Boat." The adventure in the dinghy was a dramatic real-life enactment of a theme that runs through his work from the earliest Asbury Park reports—the plight of man in an alien and indifferent universe.

In the story, Nature is sometimes cruel and deadly, sometimes beautiful and picturesque—and sometimes merely indifferent to the fate of the four men in the boat. At one moment, the unnamed narrator is in the boat, his vision narrowed to the threat of the "slaty wall of waves." At another, he seems to observe the boat and men from afar, sadly, even mockingly.

Marvelous images sustain the story's ironic tension. Sea gulls are "uncanny and sinister" and "somehow gruesome and ominous" as they stare at the men with "black beadlike eyes." Another time, seen "in slanting

Crane, a skilled horseman, riding in Florida while en route to Cuba to cover a revolution, 1896

George Arents Research Library,
Syracuse University

flight up the wind toward the gray desolate east," they represent not Nature's anger but her beauty, order, and harmony. There is "the terrible grace of the waves." A shark is "an agent of nature's inscrutable malice," yet "the speed and power of the thing was to be greatly admired."

In the end, the man accepts the "serenity of nature amid the struggle of the individual. . . . She did not seem cruel to him then, nor beneficent, nor treacherous, nor wise. But she was indifferent, flatly indifferent."

Crane tried to find another way to get to Cuba, but by mid-March he was about to give up and wrote to brother William: "I have been for over a month among the swamps further South wading miserably to and fro in an attempt to avoid our derned U.S. Navy. And it can't be done. I am through trying. I have changed all my plans and am going to Greece."

War threatened between Greece and Turkey. Crane looked forward to seeing his first real battle and wrote to a friend: "I am going to Greece for the *New York Journal,* and if *The Red Badge* is not all right I shall sell out my claim in literature and take up orange growing."

Six

In New York en route to Greece, Crane visited Linson. The artist was surprised to see his friend's appearance. "It was a new Stephen, almost, who confronted me, by contrast a rather dandified Steve. His hair was precisely brushed, his mustache much more than a mere shading, a well-fitting suit showing a trim well-set figure, his shoes shined and whole. He was now a bit over twenty-five. Yes, another Stephen."

Crane told him about Cora, that she would join him, and as soon as she could get a divorce, they would be married in England. She was going to cover the war for the *New York Journal* as Imogene Carter, the world's first woman war correspondent. Crane and Linson had a farewell dinner, little knowing it was the last time they would see each other. Chronically short of money, Crane sold "The Open Boat" to *Scribners Magazine* for three hundred dollars. Because he had lost the seven hundred dollars in gold in the shipwreck, he needed more for his expenses in Greece. He borrowed from McClure, giving him as collateral first option on his short stories, as well as the book rights to "The Open Boat."

He spent one of his last nights in New York with another *Journal* reporter, Robert H. Davis. The latter remarked that Crane would be covering a war in "that country for which the poet Lord Byron was prepared to shed his blood." Crane replied, "No man should be called upon to report a war in a country that he loves. I shall do a better job than Byron could have done. Greece means nothing to me, nor does Turkey." They had a last drink at the Hotel Imperial's bar.

"When we walked outside," Davis said, "we saw a girl emerge from the shadows of the Sixth Avenue El. Crane tossed his cigarette away and made a most gallant bow. I have never seen a more exquisite gesture of chivalry than this youth sweeping the pavement with his black felt. With great delicacy, as if addressing someone lost in the city, he asked the streetwalker, 'A stranger here?' 'Well,' she said, 'suppose I am a stranger. Can you show me anything?' 'Yes,' said Crane, 'I can show you the way out, but if you prefer to remain——' The street-walker said, 'You shouldn't hang out here, kid,' and sauntered off under the El. Crane looked at her as if he had seen his own Maggie and said, 'This is a long canyon. I wonder if there is a way out.' "

Crane, it seems, could court innocent young women only in his fiction. According to reporter John N. Hilliard, "Again and again he brought a lady of the streets to his room. When he lived in a boarding house that was really nothing more than a brothel, the prostitute was right down the hall. . . . All the women in his life—except Helen Trent and Nellie Crouse [whom he knew in New York in 1895]—were experienced older women like Lily Munroe, childless and later separated from her husband; Amy Leslie, an actress; Cora Taylor, a Madame; or prostitutes."

Ernest McCread, another reporter, said, "Crane took up with many a drab and was not particular as to her age, race or color." The evidence of his sex life clouds the legend of the "romantic Crane." Later, in 1898, while in Cuba, he began a novel about a boy prostitute, a subject rarely touched for at least another fifty years. He called it *Flowers in Asphalt* and aimed to make it longer than anything he had yet done. But he destroyed what he had written, along with his erotic verse, and never told anyone why.

Linson said that Crane talked about women only in admiring terms. "His was a fine nature, and his appreciation of the charm and frankness of true womanhood and the innocence of young girlhood was chivalry itself. He was also sometimes a smart-alec and an irresponsible heel. I sometimes thought that Steve was perhaps the most complete example of a self-absorbed ego . . . and as irresponsible, sometimes, as a goat, yet those shortcomings would no sooner be apparent than they would be wiped out by the very charm of his personality and honesty of intent."

"Crane never tried to hide his relationships with prostitutes," said Hilliard. Crane lived his own free life. In the slums, he found what he was looking for—the real, naked facts of life and was tolerant and absolutely unashamed. He had contempt for the hypocrisy of "respectable" people. "He had a gay spirit, was generous, liked the fleshpots and all-night poker," added Hilliard. "Of course, he must have shocked his relatives."

On March 20, 1897, Crane sailed for Europe on the *Etruria*. Cora sailed on another ship with a Mrs. Reudy, who had been with her at the Hotel de Dream. In London the women stayed out of sight while Crane was lionized by the English literary world. The *Critic*, a literary magazine, said Crane "impressed by extreme and refreshing modesty." Harold Frederic and the flamboyant journalist Richard Harding Davis honored Crane with lunch at the Savoy Club. Davis, going to Greece for the *London Times*, quickly understood Crane's relationship with Cora. "She is a peroxide blonde," he wrote home, "who has run away from her husband to be with Crane. She is a commonplace dull woman old enough to be his mother." Nothing of his nasty judgment was true.

Crane had a brief stay with Cora in Paris, then went alone to Marseilles. He sailed on April 3 on the *Guadania* for Athens, Greece, via the island of Crete. The two women traveled overland on the Orient Express from Paris to Vienna, then to Greece via Constantinople (present Istanbul), Turkey. At Crete, Crane saw the English, French, and Italian warships trying to keep peace between the island's Greeks and Turks.

Crane in 1897, covering the war between Greece and Turkey for the New York Journal

Clifton Waller Barrett Collection,
Alderman Library, University of Virginia

In Athens on April 7, he found the city charged with war fever. He wrote to William: "The reputation of my poor old books has reached Greece, and certain officials have assured me that I will be offered a position on the staff of Crown Prince Constantine. Won't that be great? I am so happy over it I can hardly breathe. I shall try like blazes to get a decoration out of the thing." One of Crane's faults, when unchecked by his usual irony, was a sense of the "grand"—and he was hoping for personal military glory.

Turkey declared war on Greece on April 17, and Crane left the next day for Epirus in the northwest. He witnessed some guerrilla attacks on the Turks but was looking for some large-scale action. He heard rumors of heavy fighting in Thessaly in the northeast and returned to Athens. About to leave for Thessaly, he was told the Greek army there had suffered defeat and had fled south in disorder.

Cora was now in Athens and determined, despite objections by Greek authorities, to get to the front. On April 29, Crane, Cora, Davis, and John Bass, chief of the *New York Journal* staff, left for Volo by boat and carriage. Crane came down with dysentery there and while Cora tried to interview the crown prince, Davis and Bass went on to Velestino "much relieved," Davis wrote, "to be free of them. He seems a genius with no responsibilities of any sort to anyone." On May 4, the Turks launched a major attack on Velestino. The next day, Crane, still weak, Cora, and a Greek servant rode twelve miles by horse to the battle area.

Cora Crane as a New York Journal *correspondent during the war between Greece and Turkey, 1897*

Clifton Waller Barrett Collection,
Alderman Library, University of Virginia

"Crane came up for fifteen minutes," wrote Davis, "and wrote a thirteen-hundred-word story on that. He was never near the front, but don't say I said so. He would have come but he had a toothache which kept him in bed. It was hard luck, but on the other hand, if he had not had that woman with him he would have been with us and not at Volo and could have seen the show toothache or no toothache. There is nothing to be said about what Crane did on the battlefield of Velestino. He ought to be ashamed of himself." Crane admitted that in the first day and a half of combat, "some other correspondents saw more than I did."

John Bass didn't like Crane, either, but his comments were far kinder than Davis's:

> He was indifferent to Turkish bullets. I sought shelter in a trench and cautiously watched the pale, thin novelist as he seated himself on an ammunition box amid the shower of shells and casually lighted a cigarette. This vast noise did not overwhelm him. He sat with a quiet expression and watched the artillerymen as they loaded and fired. . . . He complains that he cannot understand the Turks—they seem "unreal, shadows on the plains, vague figures in black, indications of a mysterious force!" A little thing like that ought not to stand in the way. Mr. Crane and the Turks should be introduced to each other, as the acquaintance would be of mutual advantage.

Another correspondent said, "The realities of war hampered Crane's imagination, his gift of picturing reality. But he wrote some superb journalism on the war."

Crane (left) *and John Bass, his fellow* New York Journal *correspondent in the Greece–Turkey war, 1897*
Clifton Waller Barrett Collection,
Alderman Library, University of Virginia

One dispatch described Greek troops coming up a mountain road under fire in the deceptively spare style Hemingway is supposed to have invented:

> Reserves coming up passed a wayside shrine. There the men paused to cross themselves and pray. A shell struck the shrine and demolished it. The men in the rear of the column were obliged to pray at the spot where the shrine had been.

On May 6, the Greek army began to retreat. Velestino was under heavy Turkish fire as Crane and Cora caught the last train out. When they reached Volo, Turkish troops were approaching the town, but they managed to get aboard a military ship bound for Athens. A few days later, though, Crane returned to the front at Domokos. But the war was lost, an armistice signed on May 20. Exhausted and ill, Crane was bedridden in Athens, but he was satisifed that war was as he had imagined. "The *Red Badge* is all right," he said. He joined Cora in London on June 10.

There, he was surprised to find an English edition of his latest novel, *The Third Violet*. He had written the book in only two months in 1896 and never had much confidence in it. When he mailed the manuscript to Appleton, he had written: "I am not sure that it is any good. It sometimes seems clever and sometimes it seems nonsensical. I've an idea it won't be accepted. It's pretty rotten work. I used myself up in the accursed *Red Badge*." Crane was right. It was probably his worst book.

The Third Violet has elements of autobiography. Crane attempted to weave together his love affairs with Helen Trent and Lily Munroe and his experiences among art students. Billy Hawker, a poor artist, is in love with Grace Fanhall, an aristocratic young lady he meets during the summer. She is wealthy but unaffected and warm. Hawker, however, feels inferior to her. Their pleasant summer relationship continues in the city, but they live in two different worlds. On three occasions, she gives him a violet as a sign that she cares for him. After he receives the second violet, he thinks the relationship should end and goes to her elegant home. She offers him the third violet. He says, "Don't pity me." Angry, she cries, "Oh, do go! Please!" Hawker realizes for the first time that she is sincere. The novel ends with—"[L]ater she told him that he was perfectly ridiculous."

American critics dismissed the book as a trifle. Some English, however, admired it. The *Academy* said that "the impression of the author as a genius is confirmed. . . . He is now in the front ranks of English and American writers of fiction." The *Atheneum* thought the book made Crane more the rival of Henry James than Rudyard Kipling, to whom he had been compared.

Crane had tried to write a charming love story but failed. H. G. Wells, one of Crane's greatest admirers, observed: "The emotions of the lovers go on behind the curtains of Crane's style, and all the enrichments of imaginative appeal that make love beautiful are omitted." The English magazine *Queen* reviewed it "only because it is written by the author of that formidable *The Red*

Badge of Courage. There is scarcely plot in *The Third Violet* . . . and [we] hope that it will be the last of its kind, and that instead of violets Mr. Crane will give us war— war—war."

Crane may already have decided to settle in England. It was clear to him that he could not live in New York or Port Jervis with Cora. Her husband had refused to give her a divorce. Perhaps he was also swayed by the warm attention and appreciation of the English literary establishment. With Harold Frederic's help, he rented a house called Ravensbrook in Surrey, a few miles southwest of London. It was a pretentious suburban brick house and he came to hate it.

A number of literary people lived nearby: the critic Edward Garnett and his wife, Constance, already a renowned translator of the works of Russian novelists; Ford Madox Ford; Robert Barr, who one day would be asked to finish Crane's last novel; and Harold Frederic. Crane met some of the greatest writers of his time: William Butler Yeats, Henry James, George Bernard Shaw, Algernon Swinburne, and Arnold Bennett. Most important was his meeting with Joseph Conrad, a friend and confidant until Crane's death.

Ford at first disliked Crane, thought him arrogant. But in later years he spoke of him as "an Apollo with starry eyes," a man who "did not seem to have the motives of common clay," and whose writings had "something of the supernatural. He comes back to me as always joyous. There are few men I have liked—nay, indeed, revered—more than Crane. He was so frail and so courageous, so preyed upon and so generous, so weighed down by misfortunes and so erect in his carriage. And he was such a beautiful genius." On the battlefield in World War I, Ford read *Red Badge* by candlelight and was so entranced "that when I left the tent at dawn, I was shocked to find men wearing khaki. The hallucinations of Crane's book had been so strong on me that I had expected to see them dressed in Federal Blue."

For months England seemed ideal to Crane. His work was admired by men whose opinions he valued. His liaison with Cora, even after it became vaguely known that she had a "past," was accepted without prejudice. But in a poignant letter to his brother William, Crane blamed himself for being an unwilling expatriate and yearned for the security of American village life: "I have managed my success like a fool and a child, but then it is difficult to succeed gracefully at 23. However I am learning every day. I am slowly becoming a man. My idea is to come finally to live at Port Jervis or Hartwood. I am a wanderer now and I must see enough but—afterwards—I think of those towns."

He hadn't yet told his family about Cora, and how she figured in his plan he didn't say. If he sounded conventional in the letter, he was still deeply unconventional. He loved to play the rough western barbarian for writers and intellectuals. "Superficially, he was harsh and defiant enough," said Ford. "His small tense figure and his normal vocabulary were those of the Man of Action of Dime Novels. He was very handy with a revolver. Indeed, he loved to sit about in breeches, leggings and shirtsleeves, with a huge Colt strapped to his belt." Ford noted the contradictions in Crane's personality. "He was also a great and elf-like writer, more otherworldly than any human soul I have ever encountered."

Crane and sociable, luxury-loving Cora had already started the pattern of high living and entertaining they couldn't really afford. Uninvited visitors came down from London—journalists, novelists, would-be poets, theater people—drawn by Crane's fame and generous hospitality. And everything—mountains of food, fine wines and whiskeys, flowers, etc.—were bought on credit. In a few short months, Crane was already two thousand dollars in debt, a considerable amount at that time. There was little money coming in, and local merchants dunned him for payment. He wrote urgent letters to his American agent, Paul Reynolds, pleading for money from any source—sales, advances, loans. "In one way Steve and I are the same person," Cora once said. "We have no sense of money at all." Crane would live under the burden of crushing debt for what remained of his life.

William Heinemann, the English publisher for both Crane and Joseph Conrad, brought them together at lunch on October 15, 1897. "We shook hands," said Conrad, "with intense gravity and a direct stare at each other, after the manner of children told to make friends." But as he had expected, "there was an instant meeting of minds." He remembered thinking as he read *Red Badge*, "Here is a man who may understand," and gave it a marvelous review:

"This is the work of an artist, of a man not of experience but a man inspired, a seer with a gift for rendering the significant on the surface of things, and with an incomparable insight into primitive emotions, who, in order to give us the image of war, had looked so profoundly into his own breast. . . ."

After Heinemann left, the two men sat in the restaurant until late afternoon, then tramped the London streets discussing writers. They were a curious pair—the small, sensitive but uneducated American, and the sophisticated, well-read Polish-born Conrad.

"I was fourteen years older," Conrad later said, "but I can write and talk to him as though we had been born together at the beginning of things."

They stopped for tea and a late supper, already close friends. At eleven that night, Conrad said, they parted "with just a handshake—no more—with no arrangements for meeting again. It struck me that we had not even exchanged addresses, but I was not uneasy. Sure enough, I soon received a postcard asking whether Crane might come to see us."

Conrad understood him from the start. "I discovered very early in our acquaintance that Crane had not the face of a lucky man. He had a quiet smile that charmed and frightened one. It made you pause because it revealed a shadow. It was the smile of a man who knows that his time will not be long on this earth."

They admired each other's work. When Crane praised his *Nigger of the Narcissus*, Conrad wrote, "If I feel depressed about the book I think, 'Crane liked the damn thing'—and I am greatly consoled. When he read "The Open Boat," Conrad wrote Crane:

"You are an everlasting surprise. You shock—and the next moment you give the perfect artistic satisfaction. Your method is fascinating. You are a complete impressionist. The illusions of life come out of your hand without a flaw. It is not life—which nobody wants—it is art, which everyone wants, mostly without knowing it."

That autumn, Crane wrote three classic short stories. "The Bride Comes to Yellow Sky" is a seemingly innocent, gentle tale, Crane spoofing the legend of the Wild West. Its main characters are a town marshal and a drunken bad man. The marshal arrives back in Yellow Sky with his new bride. The gunslinger challenges him, but the marshal says he is unarmed—and married. The bad man, stopped cold with astonishment, holsters his weapon and walks away. The marshal—unarmed and married—has broken the code each had lived by. The bad man understands that he is now a relic. Polite civilization has changed the lawless West. It was the end of an era—soon to be followed by church choirs, temperance meetings, schoolmarms, the closing of the open range and the frontier.

Conrad thought the story charming and telling, but it was the other two that gripped him and confirmed Crane's genius.

"The Blue Hotel" is the story of a half-crazed Swede. He arrives in a Nebraska town during a blizzard, his head filled with fantasies of western violence. At his hotel, which is painted a screaming shade of blue, he is certain that the harmless men are desperadoes who want to kill him. In a card game, he gets into an argument with the son of the hotel keeper. The two go out into the storm to fight, and the Swede beats up the young man. Boasting in the local saloon, he invites the local gambler and his poker cronies to drink with him. When the gambler refuses, the Swede seizes him by the throat. There is a struggle and the Swede is knifed, crashing to the floor with "a cry of supreme astonishment." Like some of Crane's earlier characters, the Swede is victimized by an overpowering conceit, or false pride. Having beaten the blizzard, he feels invulnerable to what he sees as the lawless West. Like *Red Badge* and "The Open Boat," the story is fired by one of Crane's deepest obsessions— man's alienation in a world ruled by irrational forces— the chief one man's own distorting pride.

"The Monster" is a study of village hysteria and social cruelty. Dr. Trescott's black stableman, Henry Johnson, rescues Trescott's son from the burning house. But Johnson has been badly burned by laboratory chemicals, his face destroyed. The grateful doctor saves the stableman, despite a judge's advice to let him die. Johnson becomes the village monster, no longer a hero. He arouses fear and hatred in people, even other blacks, who resent the doctor for having saved Johnson. They demand that he send the black man to an institution, and when Trescott refuses, they cruelly shun him and his family.

No white American author before Crane had featured a black performing a truly heroic act. Using a story of a stock comic figure (of those times) who breaks the stereotype by his heroism, Crane indicted the crowd mentality that must crush what it cannot understand.

Harold Frederic said the story was so offensive it should be thrown away. A friend of Crane's wrote that "for years I was troubled by the memory of the black man's shattered face and, reading the tale after Crane died, was surprised to find that all my horror had been excited by the simple statement 'He had no face.' " Conrad thought it a masterpiece, but something about Crane troubled him and he wrote to Edward Garnett:

> He is strangely hopeless about himself. . . . His eye is very individual and his expression satisfies me artistically. His temperament is curiously unique. His thought is concise, connected, never very deep—yet often startling, with his rapidity of action. Why is he not immensely popular? With his strength, with that amazing vision—why is he not? He ought to go very far—but will he? I sometimes think that he won't. It is not an opinion, it is a feeling. I could not explain why he disappoints me—why my enthusiasm withers as soon as I close the book. While one reads, of course, he is not to be questioned. He is the master of his reader to the very last line—then—apparently for no reason at all—he seems to let go of his hold. It is as if he grips you with greased fingers. His grip is strong, but while you feel the pressure on your flesh you slip out of his hand—much to your own surprise.

Many years later the critic Alfred Kazin also expressed some doubts about Crane:

"For all its beauty, Crane's work was curiously thin. . . . His desperation exhausted him too quickly, his unique sense of tragedy was a monotone. . . . But though he gave the 1890s a sudden direction and a fresher impulse, he could contribute no more than the intensity of his spirit."

Seven

Conrad and his family visited Crane at Ravensbrook in February 1898. Crane proposed that they collaborate on a play with an American western background. "I am afraid that would be cheating you," Conrad said. "I have no dramatic gift, whereas you have terseness, a clear eye, and an easy imagination. My ideas fade—yours come out sharp as cameos—they bring images and light. You need no help. Why should you share your power with me?" But Conrad was fascinated by the idea of working with a talent as mercurial as Crane's. "If you should really, honestly, artistically think I could be of some use . . ." The collaboration came to nothing.

That same month, the U.S. battleship *Maine* exploded in the harbor of Havana, Cuba. There was talk of war between the United States and Spain, but Crane hardly seemed to notice. He was busy writing and socializing and had found a new fascination. Inexorably drawn to the seedy and criminal, he often went to London to roam the streets of Whitechapel and Limehouse in the city's East End. But when there was a formal declaration of war in April, Crane could talk of little else. He asked Conrad for a loan to get him back to New York. "He wanted it before the sun set, before dinner, at once that instant—lest peace be declared and the opportunity of seeing a war be missed," said Conrad. "Nothing could have held him back. He was ready to swim the ocean." Conrad got the money from Blackwood and Company, a London publisher, but he had to pledge his future work against the loan.

"I have raised the wind and sail tomorrow," Crane wrote to a friend who had loaned him another fifty dollars. "Shall get myself taken in the Navy if possible." He left one hundred dollars of the borrowed money with Cora to pay some debts. But when the creditors found out he was gone, they obtained judgments against her. She fled to Ireland to live with friends for a few weeks. When she returned to England, she closed Ravensbrook and rented a London flat. Feeling abandoned and lonely, she still made plans for an even more lavish house. Crane, she thought, would be enthusiastic about it.

Crane sailed to New York on the *Germanic*, arriving on April 21. Unable to pass the navy's physical examination, he signed on as a war correspondent for three thousand dollars with the *New York World*. The *World* and William Randolph Hearst's *Journal* had inflamed public feeling against Spain by distorting and slanting the news from Cuba. Crane was in Key West, Florida, by April 26. He was one of 150 correspondents crowding the hotels, impatiently waiting for action. Sylvester Scovel, who had been with Crane in Greece, was in charge of the *World*'s two dispatch boats, *Triton* and *Three Friends*.

Some of the most brilliant and daring newspapermen in America were in Key West. Crane knew that his chief rival would be Richard Harding Davis. They had had an uneasy relationship in Greece, and Davis was now even more celebrated. The artist Charles Dana Gibson used Davis as the model for the male counterpart of his famous Gibson Girl, the ideal young American woman. Davis's square-jawed, clean-cut, pink-cheeked good looks were considered the ultimate in manly appeal. His character was what used to be called "muscular Christianity." He and Crane could hardly have been less alike.

On May 1, 1898, Admiral George Dewey's U.S. Asiatic Fleet defeated the Spanish at Manila Bay in the Philippine Islands. The victory inspired Theodore Roosevelt, then assistant secretary of the navy, to resign and form the first volunteer cavalry. It was the regiment of cowboys, Ivy League sportsmen, and assorted adventurers called the "Rough Riders." There was a great surge of patriotism—and nasty jingoism—in America. It became a war of slogans: Remember the *Maine* . . . A Splendid Little War . . . Our Little Brown Brothers. The war was *the* story of the moment, and editors were desperate for copy. Crane later wrote:

"We were fought by our managing editors tooth and nail . . . and we were urged to remember that the American people were a collection of super-nervous idiots who would immediately have convulsions if we did not throw them some news—any news. The news that arrived in Key West from Cuba as a mouse was cabled north as an elephant."

While Crane was in Key West, Doubleday published his first collection of short stories: *The Open Boat and Other Stories*. Heinemann's English edition was published at the same time, adding nine of his New York sketches. The book was received as an important literary event. The *Spectator* called him "the most striking and irresistible of all the younger American writers."

In the first months of the war, Crane was in and out of Key West. His dispatch boat trailed navy patrols blockading the Cuban coast. They waited for Spanish Admiral Cervera's fleet to arrive from Europe to give battle. Crane was on Admiral William Sampson's flagship when it ran the northwest coast of Cuba to search out gun batteries. Throughout May, he was at sea for days at a time, tracing the Cuban coast, touching at Haiti or Jamaica to send dispatches from cable staions there. The dispatch boats were often in the way of the warships and were dangerously challenged. One Crane dispatch described the *Triton*'s encounter with the U.S. gunboat *Machias*, which almost ran the tug down in a scary night action. Another time, the cruiser *St. Paul* mistook the dispatch boat for a Spanish gunboat and chased it down in a harrowing sea run. But somehow Crane still found time to write fiction. He began his Whilomville stories about his boyhood.

Crane aboard the Three Friends *off Cuba as* New York World *correspondent during the Spanish-American War, 1898*
Beinecke Rare Book and Manuscript Library,
Yale University

Novelist Frank Norris was aboard the *Triton* on one of its cruises and described Crane:

"He was wearing a pair of duck trousers grimed and fouled with all manner of pitch and grease and oil. His shirt had no collar or scarf and was unbuttoned at the throat. His hair hung in ragged fringes over his eyes. . . . Between his heels he held a bottle of beer against the rolling of the boat, composing obscene lyrics to old sea chanteys. . . . I wonder what readers of his war novel, who rightly hold him to be a great genius, would have thought had they seen him at this moment."

When in Key West, Crane usually gambled and drank or stayed to himself. Many correspondents didn't like him. He seemed aloof, sometimes arrogant and indifferent. But even though Richard Harding Davis disliked Crane, he saw his worth. After the war, he wrote that Crane was the best correspondent in the field, despite his lack of discipline and his unconventional behavior. Sylvester Scovel's wife, Frances, was in Key West. She had never been impressed by Crane, "a quicksilver personality, a queer little man with much ego," but she was angry that none of the correspondents seemed to grasp that Crane was a sick man. A former nurse, she recognized the peculiar glassy color of the whites of his eyes as a sign of tuberculosis. And she was convinced that his "out of the world" manner that others took for a mild drunken buzz was a symptom of Crane's illness.

Crane witnessed the shelling of Matanzas by Admiral Sampson's flagship. After the U.S. Navy made an attempt to sink a Spanish ship in the Santiago harbor with a "floating bomb"—a coaling ship loaded with explosives—correspondents headed for Haiti to file the story. They found the cable office closed because the army was putting down a revolution. Crane and the army commander were soon the best of friends and the cable office was opened.

"Crane hadn't bathed in weeks," said Ernest McCready, a *Herald* correspondent, "his breath was foul, yet to our amazement he was the center of attention everywhere he went. Laughing children followed him, the general thought him a capital fellow, and he was continually approached by pretty young women, disappearing with several for long stretches of time. In the excitement he never got around to writing anything about the Santiago action."

On June 10 he saw his first land action at Guantánamo Bay. A force of 650 marines, singing "There'll Be a Hot Time in the Old Town Tonight," established a base camp on the high ground overlooking the harbor. That evening, Crane went ashore with the last group of marines while other correspondents sailed to Jamaica to cable their stories. McCready said Crane stayed behind "because he expected much personal enjoyment. A hawser cable could not have dragged him away." Crane was sick with malaria but determined to stick it out. He often went to the hospital tent to get quinine and talked to Assistant Surgeon John B. Gibbs, joking about the light Spanish resistance. One night, as he approached the tent, the Spanish launched a strong surprise attack. Crane dropped to the ground as rifle fire cracked, but

Gibbs, standing in the light of the tent, was hit in the head, mortally wounded.

"For a moment," Crane wrote, "I was no longer a cynic. I was a child who, in a fit of ignorance, had jumped into the vat of war."

Lying in the dark, he could hear the dying surgeon gasping for breath.

"He was dying hard. It took him a long time to die. . . . He was going to break . . . every wave, vibration, of his anguish beat upon my senses. He was long past groaning . . . there was only the bitter struggle for air which pulsed out in a penetrating whistle, with intervals of terrible silence. . . . I thought this man would never die. I wanted him to die. Ultimately he died."

Two days later, Crane went out with a marine force to destroy an enemy position at Cuzco. The unit came under intense sniper fire. Crane was impressed by brave signalmen standing exposed to enemy fire while calmly wigwagging semaphore flag messages to a gunboat off the coast. His superb account of the action—headlined by the *World*: THE RED BADGE OF COURAGE WAS HIS WIG-WAG FLAG—was judged one of the best dispatches of the war. He actually was in the fighting himself, acting as a sort of informal adjutant to the commander of the raid and was cited in official reports for gallantry under fire.

Crane's health soon worsened from the rigors of the war, but he obsessively looked for the most grueling and dangerous missions. A few days after Cuzco, he went ashore with Scovel and another correspondent on an expedition into the mountains behind Santiago. They intended to spy on Admiral Cervera's fleet bottled up in the harbor by American ships. They rode horseback "infernal miles" through rugged country and scaled a two-thousand-foot mountain overlooking Santiago. While the exhausted Crane rested, Scovel made sketches of the black-hulled enemy ships in the harbor far below. On June 22, Crane was at Daquiri and Siboney when the main American army landed for an assault against Santiago over the San Juan Heights. Crane and Richard Harding Davis were with Roosevelt's Rough Riders. Despite his differences with Roosevelt in the Dora Clark affair, Crane admired him for leaving a soft government post to fight in a war. Roosevelt, however, never said a word to Crane. He much preferred a man like Richard Harding Davis—they were both versions of the perennial American boy. He also had no patience with Crane's introspective and creative reporting, and later said, "I did not see any sign among the fighting men, wounded or unwounded, of the very complicated emotions assigned to their kind by a certain novelist who has written about battles."

Crane became uneasy at the contrast between the professionalism of the marines and the boisterous Rough Riders who "think they are on a picnic," he said, "babbling joyously, arguing, joking and laughing, making more noise than a train going through a tunnel." One day, Crane and Davis found Edward Marshall, a *Journal* correspondent, shot in the spine and sitting propped against a tree beside a jungle trail. They moved him to a dressing station, and then Crane took the rough trail back to Siboney to notify *Journal* men to file Marshall's dispatches. On June 29, Crane and Davis were at El Pozo below the Spanish fortifications when General William Shafter launched his attack.

They watched the Rough Riders, on foot, capture Kettle Hill (not, as the legend has it, San Juan Hill a mile distant). Up on El Pozo, someone shouted, "By God! There go our boys up the hill!" Crane felt "a thrill of patriotic insanity . . . yes, yes they were going up the hill." This was the famous charge up "San Juan Hill," which would propel Roosevelt to the presidency. Later, illustrators and writers would supply the heroic elements missing from the actual scene—the gleaming bayonets, upraised sabers, men on horseback. Actually, Roosevelt had ignored orders and pushed on ahead of the Tenth Negro Cavalry, and his men were accused, in their rush and excitement, of firing on American soldiers.

The battle surged to the top of San Juan ridge. Crane, Davis, Colonel Leonard Wood, and Jimmy Hare, *McClure's* magazine photographer, lay low under the heavy fire. Crane suddenly stood up and moved to the crest of the ridge.

"Get down!" shouted Wood. "You're drawing fire on these men."

Crane seemed not to hear.

"What's the idea?" shouted Hare. "Did you get a wire from your boss, reading 'Why don't *you* get wounded so we can get some notices too'?"

Crane still didn't move and Davis called out—"You're not impressing anyone by doing that, Crane."

Crane dropped down.

"I knew that would get you," said Davis.

Crane grinned. "Oh, was that it?"

Davis later said that he thought Crane had a death wish and had deliberately tried to get himself killed a number of times.

Only moments before his show of bravado, Crane had been deeply shaken when he saw Reuben McNab, an old Claverack classmate, lying on the San Juan trail with a bad chest wound. When McNab saw Crane, he said only, "Well, they got me," and died.

McCready and many other correspondents admitted they were scared under fire. "But Crane wasn't," said McCready. "He had no fear in him as far as battle, murder, or sudden death was concerned—that's the way everyone thought who was with him in places where men get their wind up. . . . You see, Crane was an artist from crown to heel, undisciplined, careless of any interest but his own private ones. If he took chances, that was him. It's hogwash that he tried to get himself killed."

A *London Daily Chronicle* correspondent who was at Cuzco and San Juan later wrote in an obituary for Crane:

In 1898 he looked more like a boy of eighteen than a young man of twenty-six. With his fragile physique and shy and sensitive disposition, he was the last man who might be expected to figure in the storm and stress of battle. Yet Little Stevey—as we all called him—was possessed of the highest and truest courage of a man of keen imagination, and he proved it on more than one stricken field.

A year after the war, Marine Major Charles Mc-Cawley wrote to Crane:

> I and all my brother officers look back with pleasure and pride upon your service with us in Cuba, for you were the only outsider who saw it all—and we regard you as an honorary member of the Corps.

Crane was in Jamaica on July 31, and when he returned to Cuba, he was disappointed to find that he had missed a spectacular sea battle—the destruction of Admiral Cervera's fleet when it steamed out of Santiago harbor. In Siboney, Crane became delirious, "my veins burned and boiled." An army doctor said it wasn't malaria but yellow fever. He was quickly evacuated with hundreds of wounded and sick to Fort Monroe, Virginia, aboard the *City of Washington*. He recovered quickly, and dressed in a new suit, he went to New York where he ran into unexpected trouble.

Don Seitz, the *World*'s business manager, refused his request for an advance and disallowed twenty-four dollars Crane had claimed for the new suit. "Don't you think you've had enough of Mr. Pulitzer's money without earning it? You've sent us only one dispatch of merit." Crane actually had sent about twenty-five, some still in print today, almost a hundred years later. Crane merely said, "Well, if that's the way you feel about it, bye-bye." He was also accused of disloyalty for filing a dispatch for Marshall, the wounded *Journal* correspondent. Crane never told him that it was Scovel of the *Journal* who had filed the dispatch. A year later, Davis and Marshall himself gave the lie to the *World*'s charge. Seitz never let up—he even charged Crane with "imperiling" the *World* by criticizing the conduct of the Seventy-first New York Volunteers in the fighting at San Juan (a rival paper quickly called the story "an intolerable insult to the State of New York").

Crane signed on with Hearst's *Journal* to report the Puerto Rico campaign. He made a fast trip to New York's Adirondack Mountains to consult a specialist about his lung trouble and was told there was no cause to worry. He talked to a publisher about a collection of Cuban war stories. He left for Pensacola, Florida, where he boarded the *Journal* boat just before it sailed for Puerto Rico. Charles Michelson was a correspondent on the boat— "Crane looked terribly ill, worse than he had looked at San Juan only a month before." Puerto Rico was an almost bloodless anticlimax to the war, and Crane's time there was marked only by one daring escapade.

He and Richard Harding Davis were drinking in Ponce on the first night of the occupation. Crane remarked that capturing a Puerto Rican town was so easy, a newspaperman could do it. Davis, intrigued, pulled out a map and pointed to a likely place for conquest, the town of Juana Diaz. They agreed to go there at sunrise and have plenty of time to conquer the town before the advancing U.S. Army stole the glory. But the next morning, Davis overslept. Crane wanted to wake him, but Michelson said if Davis couldn't get up in time to cover the story, that was his fault.

So, wrote Davis, "while I slumbered, Crane crept forward between the army's advance posts, and fell upon the doomed garrison." Crane appeared in the town square in a military-looking khaki suit and leggings. He was met by the mayor, who ceremoniously presented the "conqueror" with the keys to the town jail. According to Davis, Crane then lined up the town's male population and randomly divided them into "good fellows" and "suspects." The good fellows were invited to take part in a victory celebration, the suspects ordered confined to their homes. "From the window," wrote Davis, "the 'suspects' looked out with envy on the feast of brotherly love that overflowed from the plaza into the side streets and lashed itself into a friendly carnival of rejoicing. It was a long night, and it will be long remembered in Juana Diaz."

That was Davis's version. But since the prank sounded arrogant and mean spirited, unlike Crane's true character—perhaps Davis got the story wrong. Or wrote it that way to demean Crane.

Crane was in Ponce when the armistice with Spain was signed on August 12. Within days, he was back in Key West where he cabled Cora. Then, posing as a British tobacco buyer, he slipped into Havana, Cuba, via the Bahama Islands and lost himself to the world.

He found Havana a depressing and filthy city. Food was scarce, prices inflated, sanitation was primitive, and scavengers were everywhere. But it suited Crane that the city was a dead and lonely place. His Havana sketches betray a physical and emotional exhaustion, and occasional bitterness. His three thousand dollars from the

World had mysteriously disappeared, and he was still deep in debt in England. In September, he learned that the *Journal* had taken him off the payroll on the day the armistice was signed. The paper had also discontinued the payments for Cora that he had arranged. He was receiving only twenty dollars for his Havana articles and had to move from an expensive hotel, leaving a large bill, to a cheap boardinghouse. He wrote every day in a frantic, futile attempt to get out of debt. On September 10, the *Jacksonville Times-Union* printed a story saying that Crane had disappeared from his hotel and "police had been shadowing him for several days before he disappeared."

Cora hadn't heard from him since his cable. When a friend sent her the *Times-Union* story, she was frantic and fired off appeals to anyone who might help: the secretary of war, the American ambassador to Britain, the British consul in Havana, and some of Crane's friends. But all the time he was in Havana, Crane never wrote her.

Between August and November 1898, he wrote newspaper articles, wrote poems about guilt and betrayal in love, finished four Cuban war stories, and worked on *Active Service*, a novel based on his adventures in Greece. He bombarded Paul Reynolds, his American agent, with desperate appeals for money: "I have got to have at least $1,500 this month, the sooner the better. . . . For Christ's sake get me some money quick here by cable."

Crane's mysterious behavior has never been explained. He had played high stakes poker in Puerto Rico, one theory goes, and might have been running from gambling debts. Another is that he was financially and emotionally close to bankruptcy and perhaps needed time away from everything. Or he might have been black-mailed. It was during this period that Crane talked of writing a book about a boy prostitute. A friend said, "Given Stevey's record of blundering into trouble while engaged in research, he might well have become the victim of an extortionist." When Frances Scovel returned to Havana a year later, she found friends buzzing with disapproval over Crane's scandalous behavior. She said that she never found out exactly what happened because no one would discuss the details in front of her.

In November, Crane's British publisher advanced him $250, and he took the next steamer for New York. Cora, still in England, had been served summonses for debts, and Conrad tried, without success, to borrow money for her from his publisher. She was deeply hurt that she had to learn Crane was still alive from the British consul. Crane drifted to New York, unsure of where to turn next. He met Louis Senger, an old Sullivan County friend, in the city. Senger remembered that Crane joked morbidly about his poor health, saying that "they had not got to him yet." He felt that Crane "was essentially a soldier who would have elected to die in battle rather than wait for the slower death of which he had a pro-phetic knowledge."

Crane wrote a friend that he was trying to get Cora to come to New York, but she insisted he come back to England. "We are carrying on a duel at long range with ink." When finally Crane told her he had decided to go back to England, she wasn't sure she wanted him. In the end, though, she relented and was waiting for him when his ship docked. "There is no spirit of Evil," she wrote in her diary. "We are betrayed by our own passions and the chief of these passions is love. It is the nemesis that stalks the world." Nemesis was the mythological Greek goddess of punishment.

ℰight

Creditors came down on Crane as soon as he landed in England. The rent at Ravensbrook had not been paid in a year. Village merchants and London department stores pressed him for payment. Cora had tentatively rented another house, Brede Place. But their tangled legal affairs held them at Ravensbrook. Crane's English literary agent, the generous and long-suffering James B. Pinker, finally freed them by agreeing, in effect, to guarantee their debts.

Brede Place was one of England's most historic houses. Begun in 1378, in the reign of Richard II, it was a massive, gloomy, forbidding place. But when Cora showed Crane from room to room, he fell in love with it. "The realist and cynic," said Ford Madox Ford, "shared Cora's amiable romanticism." Crane thought he could use the fabulous house as background for his fiction and did in a short story and his last novel. He also saw—

*Brede Place, Crane's home in England, where he spent the last
year of his life*

through Cora's eyes—that it would give them social sta-
tus, especially important to her. But many of its stone-
vaulted rooms were crumbling and uninhabitable. There
were no modern facilities—no gas or electricity, no
plumbing, no way of heating except fireplaces. It was
famous for its ghosts and once notorious as a smugglers'
hideout. Servants from the village of Brede refused to
stay overnight in the ancient house.

They moved to Brede in February 1899 with their

growing household. Harold Frederic had died and they were caring for his two youngest children. There was also Cora's friend Mrs. Reudy, a servant, and horses and dogs. At Brede they added a butler, cook, gardener, coachman, and two maids. Incredibly, their plan had been to live cheaply. They were given the house for a token rent by the owner, Moreton Frewen, a Crane admirer. But the simplest economies were beyond the impractical and extravagant couple. Cora immediately ordered expensive embossed stationery, three hundred roses for planting in a front garden, and an architect's survey for repairs and restorations to the house.

Crane and Conrad bought a boat. But Crane soon defaulted in his share of the monthly payment. "I'm so sorry Stephen worried about the money," Conrad wrote Cora. "I sent a check in his name yesterday." Months later, Conrad was "speechless" when Cora suggested that Crane's half share in the boat be taken over by their wood merchant "in payment of our account." The wood bill went unpaid and Conrad had to pay the owner of the boat the rest of the money.

In 1924 young Hayton Preston, an American interested in Crane, was directed to Brede Place by an old woman. When he said, "Mr. Crane lived here, I think?" her eyes grew hard. "He did—the rotter!" Preston was shocked but she went on: "Yes, he is a rotter. He owes me twenty pounds for firewood!" Preston said, "Well, I'm afraid you won't get it now. He died twenty-four years ago." Her expression softened. "Yes, I suppose he must be dead, or he would have paid me." She described Crane as "a thin gentleman who rode a lot and drank some." No, she didn't know he was a writer, but she "thought he looked delicate." He was a kind man, she said, and "he certainly had a great many friends."

Crane must have been conscious of the irony of living at Brede Place, the radical individualist playing lord of the manor. He was the ex-bohemian who had cadged a bed where he could, the man who loved the sleazy Bowery, the western adventurer, and war lover. But Brede appealed to his romantic side. Some of his friends jokingly called him Baron Brede and thought he took his role as lord seriously. But he played it in his usual careless fashion, often speaking like a Bowery tough ("I'm a fly guy that's wise to the all-night push") or a man of the western plains ("Say, when I planted those hoofs of mine on Greek soil I felt like the hull of Greek literatchoor, like some hayraker gone over to the goldarn majority").

The aristocratic Henry James visited Crane. He disliked Cora, whose casual manners and careless talk grated on his nerves. He was more tolerant of Crane's quirks because of his obvious gifts. He thought his young countryman a charming and extraordinarily talented apprentice writer, working toward a brilliant future. "We love Stephen Crane for what he is. We admire him for what he is going to be." Crane, in turn, was boyishly respectful to the Master. But when James was finicky and difficult, Crane sometimes called him Henrietta Maria. The two had little in common, their temperaments and approach to art quite different. But there was mutual respect and admiration, even if James told Ford that "the

Cora Crane at Brede Place, 1899
Clifton Waller Barrett Collection,
Alderman Library, University of Virginia

surely gifted young man is wholly atrocious for accent and mannerisms."

Cora hoped that "the perfect quiet of Brede and the freedom from a lot of dear good people, who take his mind from his work, will permit that machine-like application which makes a man work steadily." To the end, Cora depended on Crane to solve their money problems, while making them worse—but he was equally guilty.

Crane in his study at Brede Place, 1899
Clifton Waller Barrett Collection,
Alderman Library, University of Virginia

Both seemed compelled to entertain and spend lavishly.
Invited guests and strangers paraded through the house,
and the sparsely furnished guest rooms were always
filled. Crane welcomed his friends at any time, but he
called the unwanted strangers "lice."

Although he wrote a friend that "we love Brede with
a wildness which I think is a little pathetic," the house
began to take its toll on him. Windswept, cold, and damp,
it was a dangerous place for a person with tuberculosis.
His doctor later said he never should have lived there,

and his friends thought Brede Place killed him. But day after day, Crane sat in his workroom and wrote merely clever stories and a novel to try and pay his debts. *Active Service* was originally meant to be a serious war story, but it became an adventure-romance for a popular audience. When he finished the book, he wrote a friend: "I must confess to you—after dismal sorrow and agony— there was born into an unsuspecting world a certain novel called *Active Service,* full and complete in all its shame . . . which same is now being sent forth to the world to undermine whatever reputation I have achieved up to this time and may heaven forgive it for being so bad." John Berryman, poet and Crane biographer, called it "a wonderfully bad, uncomfortable, stupid book."

Crane flooded Pinker with stories as he had promised. But there was always a note demanding or begging for immediate payment before the agent sold it, Crane estimating the price. Pinker replied, "I must confess, you are becoming most alarming." By this time, Pinker had advanced Crane more than one thousand dollars of his own money. Paul Reynolds, Crane's American agent, tired of Crane's incessant demands for money, had dropped him—or was dropped, as Crane hinted. Pinker became his agent for both countries.

Always desperate, Crane wrote brother William to borrow more money:

"If you think I am not hustling to get out of this hole you are mistaken. But sometimes I think I can't quite do it. Let me know as soon as you see this letter exactly what are the prospects of your sending me five hundred dollars by the first of April. We are living very quietly, devoting all our attention to my work. . . . If the month of March don't wipe me off the earth, I hope by this time next year to be fairly rich. . . ."

William decided to send his daughter Helen to England. He would pay for her board at Brede Place and for sightseeing on the Continent. Helen was one of Crane's favorites and he welcomed her . . . and the board money. They visited Switzerland and France, but he came down with an attack of malaria in Paris, and they had to return home. By the end of the summer, his financial situation steadily getting worse, he wrote only what he could finish quickly and sell immediately for cash. Among them, however, were his *Whilomville Stories*, some of his most appealing work.

Whilomville is any boy's town. Whilom means *once upon a time*. The stories are set in various towns and cities of Crane's boyhood, but mainly in Port Jervis. The town, he wrote,

drawled and drowsed through long months, during which nothing was worse than the white dust which arose behind every vehicle at blinding noon, and nothing was finer than the cool sheen of the hose sprays over the cropped lawns under the maples at twilight. . . . The main street has shimmering blue arc-lamps and the orange glare of gaslight in the shop windows. A crowd at the post office awaits the evening mail and at the corners young men gather to watch the passing scene. There is a shrill electric streetcar whose motor sings like a cageful of grasshoppers.

They were charming, humorous tales that reveal Crane's natural sympathy for children and his sharp insight into the savagery of their social codes—and of those imposed on them by adults.

In the sixteen months from the time he returned from Cuba until his final collapse, he wrote an astonishing amount: thirteen Whilomville stories; seven Cuban war stories; the last half of *Active Service*; two-thirds of *The O'Ruddy* (unfinished when he died); two western stories; four war stories about a regiment in an imaginary country; six chapters for *Great Battles of the World*; and at least thirty miscellaneous stories, sketches, and newspaper articles.

In September 1899 many of Crane's friends were already in South Africa covering the Boer War. He wrote Pinker to get him an assignment as a war correspondent—"I am getting serious about it. See if you can work it up." Cora was panic-stricken at the thought of his leaving her again. "I am so glad you told him *not* to go," she wrote Pinker. "His health is not fit for it. He had a return of Cuban fever in Paris and he is in no physical condition to stand a campaign no matter how short it may be. He has settled down to his work so well and ought not to leave home." She added a postscript: "Please don't let Mr. Crane know that I said a word against his going."

He now began to surrender to the ravages of tuberculosis, malaria, overwork, and worry. Conrad said that Crane's life "seemed altogether out of control." Crane wrote a friend for information about health resorts in

Germany's Black Forest: "The truth is Cuba just about liberated me from this base blue world. My clockwork is juggling badly. . . . I'm just a dry twig on the edge of a bonfire."

H. G. Wells wrote, "What he was still clinging to, but with dwindling zest, was artistry."

But by the end of the year, Crane was in good enough spirits to have an elaborate week-long Christmas–New Year celebration. Guests and games and dancers swirled about him, but he seemed unusually quiet and withdrawn. "He was profoundly weary and ill, if I had been wise enough to see it," said Wells, "but I thought him sulky and reserved." A guest wandering through the house found Crane sitting alone, softly strumming a single string on a guitar. As the man approached, Crane collapsed against him. During the night, he had a severe hemorrhage and Wells rode off on a bicycle to get a doctor. He recovered enough in early January to work at his desk. Cora wrote Pinker an apology for her constant demands for money and assured him that one day Crane "will prove his appreciation of your simply saving him from going smash." But three days later Crane wrote him a brutal, almost irrational, letter: "I must have the money. I cannot get on without it. If you cannot send $250 by the next mail, I will have to find a man who can. I know this is abrupt and unfair, but self-preservation forces my game with you precisely as it did with Reynolds."

Pinker telegraphed an indignant protest, and Cora assured him that Crane "intended no threat" and was "quite upset" by the agent's response. Crane immediately wrote Pinker, "I hardly know what to say further than you are a great benefit to me."

His nerves were ragged and he could be surly with unwelcome visitors: "Please have the kindness to keep your mouth shut about my health in front of Mrs. Crane hereafter. She can do nothing for me and I am too old to be nursed. It is all up with me but I will not have her scared. Mind this!"

His work was being published and he made some money. "But it all went toward keeping up that expensive house," said Conrad's wife, Jesse, "which was always filled with free-loungers—and all the while the poor man was dying. It was Cora's way of insuring that her Steve would always have a good time."

In early April 1900 Cora was shopping with Helen in Paris when she received a telegram—Crane had suffered two massive hemorrhages. She returned to Brede and ordered a specialist from London. He examined Crane for a $250 fee, pronounced his condition not serious, and left. But Crane was getting weaker by the day, suffering an abcess in the bowels and recurrent malaria attacks. Crane's local doctor, Ernest Skinner, was certain he would recover. He encouraged him to take a sea voyage and then consider settling in some dry climate in America. A friend who came to visit Crane found Cora desperate, "pacing the floor and lashing her skirt with one of his riding crops. She broke into a frantic denunciation of herself for allowing so much entertainment at Brede. . . . She finally sank into a chair, sobbing. She had

The last photograph taken of Stephen Crane
Clifton Waller Barrett Collection,
Alderman Library, University of Virginia

no real hope of his recovery. But she showed her courage
and cheered him up."

On April 21 Crane made his will, witnessed by Dr.
Skinner. He left Cora his personal belongings and—until
she married—all the income from his book royalties. But
in the end she got nothing. His brother, William, a crafty
lawyer, somehow had the will interpreted for his own
advantage.

Crane tried to put a brave face on his situation for her sake, but he was depressed about his wasted talent. He felt that he had cheated himself by doing too much hack work for money. As much as he cared for Cora, he had ambivalent feelings about her. During his illness, he wrote a poem about "a poisoned lover" who is "dying at the feet of the woman," and he describes the woman as mad. Cora, in her reckless, almost psychopathic, extravagances, almost seemed mad. He knew he was as guilty as she for agreeing to the high living . . . *but* what if he had taken up with someone more sensible? He only once confided it to Conrad, then pretended he was mocking himself. It was the regret and clear sight that came after the fall.

Sick as Crane was, he could still be concerned about a friend. Shortly before he was taken to the sanitarium, he wrote to the influential Sanford Bennett, asking him to help Conrad. "My condition is probably known to you. I have Conrad on my mind just now. He is poor and a gentleman and proud. His wife is not very strong and they have a kid. Edward Garnett says he is a great writer, but doesn't think he will ever be popular outside the ring of men who write. If Garnett should ask you to pull wires for a place for Conrad on the Civil Service list, please do me this last favor. I am sure you will." It was the last letter Crane would write.

Cora, typically, had gathered an entourage for the expensive trip to Germany. Besides herself, it included Mrs. Reudy, Helen Crane, the Brede butler, a doctor and two nurses, and Crane's favorite dog. Moreton Frewen, his landlord, and Walter Goode, a journalist friend, raised most of the money from two famous Americans: banker J. P. Morgan and industrialist Andrew Carnegie. Frewen also contributed money and paid some of Crane's debts. Conrad wrote to Cora: "You may imagine that had it been in my power to render you any sort of service I would not have waited for your appeal. I've kept quiet because I feel myself powerless. I am a man without connections, without influence and without means. . . . You can't imagine how I suffer because of my affection for Stephen and my admiration of his genius."

The first stop was at the Lord Warden Hotel in Dover on the English Channel. For days, while recouping his failing strength, Crane gazed out the window at sailboats that seemed to him "dim shadows against an iron gray sky." Conrad visited him at Dover and was shocked at his wasted look. Crane's last words to his friend were, "I am tired. Give my love to your wife and child." Conrad later told his wife, "It is the end. He knows it is all useless. He goes only to please Cora, and he rather would have died at home." Robert Barr, picked to finish *The O'Ruddy*, came and stayed four days to take notes of Crane's whispered instructions. H. G. Wells also visited and remembered "Stephen lying still and comfortably-wrapped before an open window and the calm, spacious sea." Wells was more optimistic than Conrad. "Stephen was thin and gaunt, too weak for more than a greeting and good wishes. But it did not seem to me in any way credible that he would reach his refuge in the Black Forest only to die at journey's end."

Cora still believed Crane could "get well and live for years if we can get him out of England." The party crossed to Calais, France, then by salon carriages to Boulogne and Basel, Switzerland. In Basel, they stayed at the expensive Hotel Trois Rois. From Switzerland, they went by train to Badenweiler, Germany, arriving on May 24. The money was now gone and Cora again was pleading with Pinker for money. Frewen sent $125, and Henry James $250—"It meagerly represents my tender benediction to my stricken friend."

From his corner room, Crane could see nothing but the sky. He seemed tormented by feverish dreams. "My husband's brain is never at rest," Cora wrote Frewen. "He lives over everything in his dreams and talks aloud constantly as he sleeps. It is too awful to hear him try and change places in 'The Open Boat'!"

Stephen Crane died at 3:00 A.M. on the morning of June 5, 1900, only twenty-eight years old.

"It was a brutal, needless extinction—what an unredeemed catastrophe!" Henry James wrote Cora. "I think of him with such a sense of possibilities and powers!"

Walter Goode, who had known Crane in Cuba, also wrote her:

I can't tell you how sorry I was to hear of poor Stephen's death. The world loses a man, who, as Richard Harding Davis said, was one of the few, *very* few, who possessed the spark of genius. And I lose a good friend, a man whose sincerity and bravery—a rare bravery it was, too—I admired more than I can say. And your loss—I am so sorry for you.

The obituaries hailed his genius, however unfulfilled. One of the rare negative comments came from the *New York Tribune*, where he had begun his career: "If he saw life clearly upon occasion he never saw it steadily; he never saw it whole. A sense of proportion was missing from his equipment." The *Tribune* man who wrote it was Wallace Stevens, who would become a renowned American poet. The *New York World* wrote, "He was an engaging genius, intensely human in all his impulses, lovable in his very frailties. Men lament his untimely death because he was such a fine, brave, madcap, generous comrade; women because he had the winning gift of eye and speech whose credit cannot be told in words. . . ."

Crane's body was on view at a London mortuary for a week, and in mid-June, Cora and Helen accompanied it to New York. Reverend James M. Buckley, an old friend of the Crane family, delivered the eulogy at the funeral. He said that "Stephen Crane's career was like that of a meteor which gleams brilliantly in the sky for a time and then sinks to rest."

Crane was buried in the Evergreen Cemetery in Hillside, New Jersey. The grave is marked by a large gray granite stone inscribed:

STEPHEN CRANE—POET—AUTHOR—1871–1900

After visiting the Crane family in Port Jervis, Cora returned to London. She tried, without success, to earn her living as a free-lance writer. With no buyers for her stories, she concocted endings for some of Crane's unfinished tales and sold them under his name. Still burdened by debt, she returned to America in 1901. She eventually drifted back to Jacksonville and the social underworld she had left in 1897 to follow Crane to Greece. The next year, she borrowed from friends and local bankers and built an elegant brothel she called The Court. She married Hammond McNeil, a man fifteen years her junior, the black-sheep son of a prominent family. He later accused her of adultery and shot the man he suspected was her lover. Cora had witnessed the shooting and left for England in 1907 to avoid testifying at McNeil's trial. She called on Conrad, Wells, and Frewen, but Henry James refused to see her. She returned to Jacksonville after her husband was acquitted, but the scandalous affair marked her decline. She died of a stroke in 1910 at forty-five, alone and forgotten, and was buried in Jacksonville as Cora E. Crane.

In the August 1900 issue of *North American Review*, H. G. Wells wrote of Crane's importance for the literary future. To Wells, Crane's work was a turning point in the history of imaginative writing. Crane found his most eloquent expression in images—usually moments of terror or devastation that have a riveting authenticity. Crane, Wells said, rejected the conventions and beliefs that formed the sinews of middle-class culture. His rejection of the past, the devices of nineteenth-century prose style, was radical—"As a link between the nineteenth and twentieth century, [Crane] is the first expression of the opening mind of a new period."

Crane's work and reputation were forgotten for twenty years. "I hardly meet anyone who knows or remembers anything of him," Conrad said bitterly in 1912. Wells, in 1915, wrote that "America can produce such a supreme writer as Stephen Crane—the best writer of English in the last half-century. . . . But America won't own such children . . . she'll never know she had a Stephen Crane."

The resurgence of interest in Crane began with the 1923 publication of Thomas Beer's biography *Stephen Crane*. A year later the critic Carl Van Doren wrote that modern American literature began with Crane's fiction.

In his fiction and poetry Crane sees man as caught between the claims of the past and the demands of the present, a perception that is strikingly modern. New readers discovered the range and complexity of Crane's fiction and how crisp and sensory it was. In his 1950 biography of Crane, John Berryman hailed him as "one of the few manifest geniuses the country has produced." Today, Stephen Crane is recognized the world over as a great original writer, and his place in literary history is secure.

$\mathscr{B}$ibliography

Beer, Thomas. *The Mauve Decade*. New York: Knopf, 1926.

———. *Stephen Crane: A Study in American Letters.* New York: Knopf, 1923.

Bergon, Frank. *Stephen Crane's Artistry.* New York: Columbia University Press, 1975.

Berryman, John. *Stephen Crane.* New York: Sloane, 1950.

Bowers, Fredson, ed. *The Works of Stephen Crane.* 10 vols. Charlottesville: University Press of Virginia, 1969–76.

Cady, Edwin H. *Stephen Crane.* Boston: Twayne, 1980.

Colvert, James B. *Stephen Crane.* New York: Harcourt Brace Jovanovich, Inc., 1984.

Elliott, Emory, ed. *Columbia Literary History of the United States.* New York: Columbia University Press, 1988.

Hoffman, Daniel. *The Poetry of Stephen Crane.* New York: Columbia University Press, 1957.

Holton, Milne. *A Cylinder of Vision: The Fiction and Journalistic Writings of Stephen Crane.* Baton Rouge: Louisiana State University Press, 1972.

Katz, Joseph, ed. *Stephen Crane in Transition: Centenary Essays.* DeKalb: Northern Illinois University Press, 1972.

Kazin, Alfred. *On Native Grounds.* New York: Reynal and Hitchcock, 1942.

LaFrance, Marston. *A Reading of Stephen Crane.* New York: Oxford University Press, 1972.

Nagel, James. *Stephen Crane and Literary Impressionism.* State College: Pennsylvania State University Press, 1960.

Solomon, Eric. *Stephen Crane: From Parody to Realism.* Cambridge: Harvard University Press, 1972.

Stallman, R. W. *Stephen Crane: A Biography.* New York: Braziller, 1968.

Stallman, R. W., and Lillian Gilkes, eds. *Stephen Crane: Letters.* New York: New York University Press, 1960.